The Landslides in Johnson's Landing

DISASTER IN PARADISE

AMANDA BATH

**HARBOUR
PUBLISHING**

Harbour Publishing Co. Ltd.
P.O. Box 219
Madeira Park, BC, von 2h0
www.harbourpublishing.com

Edited by Holley Rubinsky and Pam Robertson
Front cover photo by Louis Bockner
Back cover photo by Renata Klassen
Map on page 9 by Roger Handling/Terra Firma Digital Arts
Index by Brianna Cerkiewicz
Text and cover design by Carleton Wilson
Printed and bound in Canada

Canada Council   Conseil des Arts
for the Arts   du Canada

BRITISH COLUMBIA
ARTS COUNCIL
An agency of the Province of British Columbia

Harbour Publishing acknowledges the support of the Canada Council for the Arts, which last year invested $157 million to bring the arts to Canadians throughout the country. We also greatfully acknowledge financial support from the Government of Canada through the Canada Book Fund, and from the Province of British Columbia through the BC Arts Council and the Book Publishing Tax Credit.

Cataloguing data available from Library and Archives Canada
ISBN 978-1-55017-695-7 (paper)
ISBN 978-1-55017-696-4 (ebook)

We dance round in a ring and suppose,
But the Secret sits in the middle and knows.

—Robert Frost

Contents

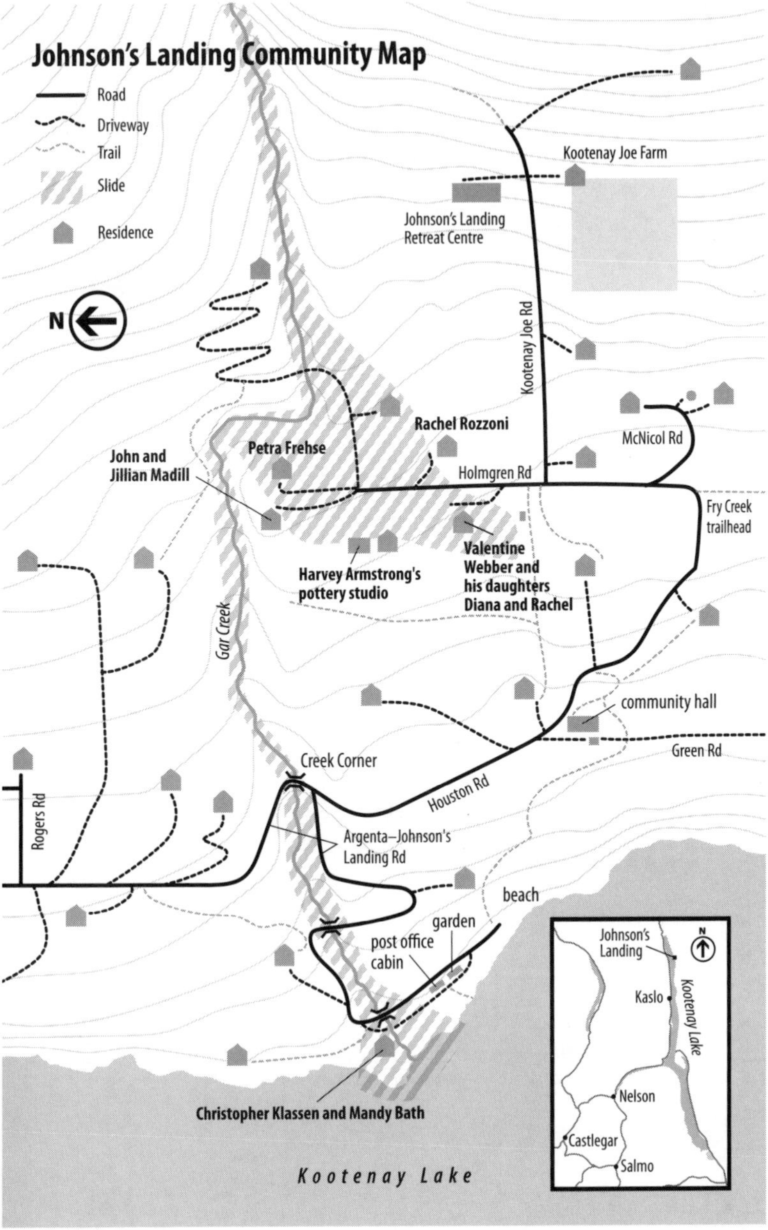
Johnson's Landing Community Map
Road
Driveway
Trail
Slide
Residence
N
Kootenay Joe Farm
Johnson's Landing Retreat Centre
Kootenay Joe Rd
Rachel Rozzoni
McNicol Rd
Petra Frehse
John and Jillian Madill
Holmgren Rd
Fry Creek trailhead
Valentine Webber and his daughters Diana and Rachel
Harvey Armstrong's pottery studio
Gar Creek
community hall
Green Rd
Creek Corner
Houston Rd
Rogers Rd
Argenta–Johnson's Landing Rd
beach
garden
post office
cabin
Christopher Klassen and Mandy Bath
Kootenay Lake
Johnson's Landing
Kaslo
Kootenay Lake
Nelson
Castlegar
Salmo

Prologue

CHRISTOPHER AND I fell in love on Manitoulin Island in Ontario, in the summer of 1992, two years after we first met at his family's summer cabin there. We sat down together on the rocky shore, as the moon scattered a pathway of diamond light towards us across Lake Huron, and made plans for our future. "Could you live in Canada, do you think?" Christopher asked me. I assured him that I most certainly could. One city was much like another, right?

"Right," he agreed. "How would it be if we moved west to British Columbia?"

I kissed him and concurred, my mind's eye already envisaging a tidy condominium apartment a bit like my home in London, England, but overlooking Vancouver and the Pacific Ocean.

Christopher went on to tell me about a place called Johnson's Landing, a remote rural community at the north end of Kootenay Lake in the southern interior of British Columbia. His sister, Renata, had just moved there with her partner, Reid, and their three daughters, and lived in a house rented from the local potter. Christopher described his sister's delight at its large, sunny gardening space, and the abundant food they grew. In my urban ignorance I wondered why they'd go to so much trouble. Surely they had shops?

As summer waned, I made decisions that shifted my life's trajectory. I decided to abandon a financially secure, intellectually rewarding research job, a home in London near my parents and the comfort of safe routines, in exchange for a much less predictable existence. We'd be travelling for a while with no fixed abode and our financial outlook was precarious. In order to work I had to apply to become a landed immigrant in Canada. Love gave me courage and I barely paused to consider the implications. I was confident of my future path beside Christopher, wherever we chose to go, and excited by the novelty of it all.

We left Manitoulin for Minnesota, where Christopher's father, Hanno, and stepmother, Julie, had their home. From there I flew to England, resigned from my job and emptied out the apartment in London. I gave away most of my possessions, stored the remainder with my parents, kissed Mummy and Daddy goodbye and was back in Christopher's embrace within eight weeks. We packed, prepared for the long road trip and, in early November, left Minnesota in the "White Whale," Christopher's Dodge van and home-on-wheels. A luxurious queen-sized mattress filled the back; as a concession to the sensibilities of his English sweetheart, Christopher put up curtains.

We crossed the border into Canada at Creston, BC, and made our way up the east shore of Kootenay Lake. The highway was winding and narrow, the day stormy and overcast. We only just made the ferry to the west side of the lake—ours was the last vehicle waved on board.

Even under heavy clouds and in the face of a biting wind, the mountain scenery was dramatic. A lifelong city girl, I'd never seen anything like this place. The lake, a one-hundred-kilometre trench of deep clean water, lies between two rugged mountain ranges: the Selkirks to the west and the Purcells to the east. Its water drains into the vast Columbia River system.

Johnson's Landing is one of the most remote communities in the West Kootenay. We drove through the village of Kaslo (population one thousand) and continued north. At the head of the lake we turned right and crossed the Lardeau River. Then another sharp right turn sent us south, once more on the east shore of the lake, beside the Argenta Flats, a wetland area and rich wildlife habitat. The road south was a gruelling twenty-two kilometres of unpaved dirt road: a juddering, corrugated dust bath in summer, and mud porridge in early spring, so Christopher told me. The road was at its best during winter freezes when snow and ice filled the ruts and potholes, and after the grader put a coat of grit overtop.

Johnson's Landing's "centre"—a community hall, a bulletin board and a bank of green mailboxes—was too small to be called a village. A broad spread of acreages extended over a bench of land above the lake and along the shoreline, ranging in size from half a hectare to just over twenty hectares, thirty-six properties all told, with some forty full-time residents. The community was named for Algot Johnson, a Swedish miner and trapper, who came to Kaslo from Colorado in around 1895. The story goes that in 1901 a storm drove his rowboat into the bay of what was to become known as Johnson's Landing, while he was out fishing. He liked what he saw, saved his money and in 1906 bought sixteen hectares of virgin wilderness on the bench of land above the shore.

We found Renata and Reid, that grey November day, in their home adjoining the Johnson's Landing pottery studio, with their daughters Rachael, Delanie and toddler Margie.

The place didn't have a single shop or amenity. What was the allure? I pondered this question a day or so later, sitting on the half-rotted dock, gazing out across the lake with not a house in sight. Maybe that was it: an attraction of opposites, a place and way of life I had never experienced or imagined. The views, the peacefulness and the spirit of the tiny community quickly convinced me. I had no hesitation telling Christopher this wild, remote place was where I wanted us to live.

OUR GREAT GOOD fortune, the following year, was to become the caretakers of a beautiful property in the Landing, a rustic lakefront house with a stunning view south towards the Salmo–Creston range. A meandering driveway crossed little Gar Creek over a tiny bridge, and led down from the house to the garden and the "post office cabin": a one-room log house dating from the 1920s that had served as the community's post office in the early days of settlement. I found a date stamp hammered into the hand-hewn cedar wall: JOHNSON'S LANDING 21 DEC 1951.

The first white settlers were farmers and orchardists who planted apples and cherries and shipped the harvest out to market on the sternwheeler ferryboat that came up Kootenay Lake once a week with the mail and provisions. There wasn't a proper road until 1957. People thought nothing of walking to and from Argenta (home to about a hundred and twenty people), seven kilometres each way, for a community event, a square dance or a celebratory meal. Life was hard work but straightforward. You either hacked it or you moved to town.

The house we lived in was built in the late 1960s by Ruth and Frank Burt, who bought the large acreage with two kilometres of waterfront from Jack Raper. After the marriage ended and Frank left the Landing, never to return in Ruth's lifetime, numerous individuals helped finish her house. Ruth was a Quaker who welcomed every passing stranger. In the late sixties and early seventies these strangers included many young men of draft age who left the United States to avoid being sent to fight in Vietnam. Evidently, more than a few of them had never wielded a hammer in their lives. The over-constructed bathroom door, for instance, was a massive jigsaw puzzle of heavy wood off-cuts, with elephant-track hammer blows around each nail.

Designed by Elmo Wolf, a disciple of Frank Lloyd Wright, the house had a pleasing upward sweep to its shed roof. Inside, the cedar plank ceiling angled up towards large picture windows that looked straight down the lake. We had what realtors call a "million-dollar view." A glory we never took for granted.

This was our paradise. We often called it that, immensely grateful for the privilege of living there. After Ruth Burt died her son was our landlord for more than a decade. Like Ruth, he endorsed our initiatives to improve the house and exterior landscaping. Always supportive and generous, he encouraged us to regard this beautiful place as our permanent home.

Returning was always a joy. We'd slide back the bar of the curious old Dutch front door that opened outwards, step over the threshold and inhale the faint cedar perfume. Enormous elk antlers hung on the wall over the staircase. We climbed four steps to the main floor: an open plan kitchen, dining and living room. Also, latterly, our bedroom, while the actual bedroom was under reconstruction.

We lived within a minute's walk of Gar Creek and the lake. I seldom crossed the bridge without stopping to pay my respects, as though before an altar. I usually looked upstream, and watched the water as it gushed towards me round the bend, under the horizontal root of an old cedar stump, and chattered onward between mossy boulders, down to the lake. Wild blackcurrant bushes nodded on the bank. The creek was, to us, a living presence with a soul, a spiritual place. We often heard voices there. I sensed its blessing as I passed on my way to the garden.

Our garden over the years became a study in driftwood and rock decoration. Christopher is an inspired landscape designer who loves to beachcomb and play with what he finds. Our garden gateposts were two upended driftwood tree trunks, their root balls standing tall like hairy-headed giants. The gate was also made of driftwood, and more pieces wove their way along the fence and marked out the garden beds.

Inside the garden, a motley collection of perennials greeted us every spring: rose bushes, clematis, phlox, hydrangeas, campanula, lilies and anemones. A grapevine crawled along the fence and Virginia creeper clambered up the gatepost. Several trees took up residence over the years, including a very fruitful mulberry, a snowball tree and an English oak grown from an acorn. I made a stab at growing vegetables but found it a bit of a struggle. The garden stood in partial shade, on top of beach gravel, and every crumb of nutritious soil had to be made or imported: compost, manure, mulch. Trying to feed the plants and prevent the beds from drying out in the August sun was a full-time task.

From Johnson's Landing we came and went. I had a small, utilitarian house in Kaslo, purchased in 2001. I was the co-ordinator of the Kaslo and Area Hospice from 1999 to 2007 and sometimes needed to spend the night "in town," as we said. Later, we rented the house out for several years but in 2012 I told Christopher I didn't want to look for another tenant, even though we'd have been glad of the income; I wanted to enjoy it myself.

Kaslo was one of the most beautiful villages I'd ever seen in British Columbia. But we always loved getting back to the Landing. It meant hearing the chuckle of water in the creek as we opened the car door, inhaling the clean forest air and, best of all, being greeted at the door by our beautiful black cat, Ozzie. He always pretended to be angry at our absence but was palpably overjoyed to see us. I would scoop him up and bury my nose in his fur. His fragrance was the reassurance and confirmation that I was back, I was home.

Ozzie, curled up on the bed where he enjoyed many morning naps.

16

Chapter 1: Countdown to Zero

IT WAS THE summer of 2012, and I'd last seen my mother, June Bath, in January when I visited her in England for three weeks. June still lived in our family home in southwest London, the house my brother and I had known since adolescence; she'd been alone there since my father's death a decade earlier. Late winter gave way to early spring and I had to face up to the fact that my mother was showing alarming symptoms of dementia. Her neighbours on either side kept an eye on her. My devoted cousin visited regularly, using all her powers of reassurance, but June sometimes phoned her more than a dozen times a day, and knocked on the neighbours' front doors late at night, agitated and confused.

I'd been going over from Canada three times a year, but my mother's needs were increasing. In late May she sounded distraught as she pleaded with me on the phone to move up my next trip, scheduled for mid-June. "Darling, I need you so badly; I don't know what's wrong; I think I'm losing my mind." I was glad my ticket was booked, and decided not to change the date; I was working almost full time. I would leave Johnson's Landing on Tuesday, June 12, and be with her on June 14.

But over the weekend, just four days before I arrived, my mother had two falls in the garden; she broke her ankle in the first and fractured her right wrist in the second. Our attentive neighbour, shocked to see June hobbling around, her ankle and wrist black and swollen, insisted on taking her to the accident and emergency department of the nearby hospital. There, the medical staff realized that something else was wrong, as my mother became increasingly frantic.

"I want to go home, I insist on being allowed to leave. You cannot keep me here against my will!" June argued her case quite plausibly at first, but then delirium took hold. She locked herself inside the ward and couldn't be persuaded to open the door for over an hour. Lacking insight into her injuries, she tottered across the room and fell down again in a vain attempt to demonstrate how mobile she was.

My mother looked pale and undernourished. The doctors held her under observation for forty-eight hours and I talked to them, en route to Vancouver airport. I made it plain that, although I was on my way, June was in no fit state to go home. Finally, the consultant geriatrician declared that my mother "lacked mental capacity." A nursing home specializing in dementia care was willing to admit her, very much against her will. On Wednesday the two nurse-managers collected her by taxi.

On Thursday morning I arrived in London, jet-lagged and disoriented. For the first time ever, my mother was not at home to greet me. The house showed tragic evidence of her struggles—she'd written her own phone number five times on the wall next to the telephone; mouldy food lay forgotten in the fridge; mail had not been opened.

The nursing home was a long bus ride away, followed by a ten-minute walk. I was impressed by its cheery, clean appearance. Exquisite arrangements of fresh flowers brightened the entrance hall; I found orchids in the bathroom. The staff were compassionate, friendly and reassuring. "We'll take good care of June. You mustn't worry." But of course I worried.

During my daily visits my mother was sometimes delusional, believing she now lived in Spain—a country she adored. On other days she thought she'd sold her house and bought the nursing home! The rooms were rather large, she confided, and she hoped the maintenance wouldn't be too much for her. On days of intense agitation she'd rip down the family photos I'd taped to her wall, empty her clothes out of the drawers and wardrobe and beg me to take her home. "You must help me, Mandy! If you leave me here, I'll die!"

But the days were running out and I knew I'd have to leave. We watched one last Wimbledon tennis match on TV together as I held her soft hand, knobbly with arthritis. My poor, darling mother was a forlorn sight, with plaster casts on her leg and forearm, her eyes puffy, her expression anxious and bewildered. She wouldn't let me leave. I had to pretend I was just popping out to the toilet.

I took a deep breath, held myself together somehow and walked out of her room without daring to look back, closing my ears to her plaintive voice calling after me, "Mandy! Darling, where are you going?" The heartache was so agonizing I could hardly breathe.

THE REST OF my family assured me I'd done the right thing but still I felt guilty and disloyal: I was a bad daughter who had let her mother down. I boarded the aircraft to Vancouver and cried inconsolably as far as Greenland, to the consternation of the flight attendant. Then I dried my eyes, blew my nose and took a deep breath. It was over. I could do no more. My mother was in good hands; the immediate worry was taken care of. I was going home. Eight hours later a tiny propeller-driven Dash-8 carried me from Vancouver to the West Kootenay's regional airport in Castlegar, towards my beloved husband, Christopher. The date was Tuesday, July 3, 2012.

Christopher picked me up in Nelson. We had five days together in the Landing before he would be leaving for Eugene, Oregon, to visit his mother. He intended to depart on Sunday, July 8, but, as usual, was twenty-four hours behind schedule. He slowly readied himself, packed the car, tidied things away and checked the tasks off his list. He worked methodically up until the last moment and slept little. He didn't want to leave; neither of us ever liked to step out from our quiet paradise into the bustling larger world. We were enchanted, held bodily under the spell of this place, and leaving took an effort of will.

That weekend Dan Miles and Gerald Garnett, friends from Kaslo, were on a multi-day kayaking trip with their wives. The men decided to kayak over to our bay Sunday morning, and stopped by for a quick visit. Delighted, we invited them in and plied them with tea, toast and eggs. We laughed and chatted in the sunlit kitchen around the old oak dining table.

After they left, one of the last tasks Christopher decided to accomplish was to set the sheets of forest green steel roofing against the side of the house, ready to be lifted into position. This was the penultimate stage of a lengthy project: re-roofing the house. The pieces were long, heavy and delicate. He used our trailer and "George," the loyal old Chevy pickup truck that belonged to our friend Paul Hunter, to bring them down to the house from the community hall where they'd been safely stored under tarps for several months. One by one we lifted each razor-edged sheet of steel and laid it onto a wooden frame Christopher had constructed, angled up against the side of the house, outside the bathroom. Almost four thousand dollars' worth of prime roofing material was carefully staged, ready for his return.

On Sunday afternoon Christopher suggested one last boat ride along the shore. We puttered north to Greg Utzig and Donna MacDonald's cabin and found Greg's boat inundated and half-submerged, filled with pebbles and driftwood; we hoisted it up the bank, clear of the exceptionally high water. Greg was a hydrologist who kept an eagle eye on Kootenay Lake levels, but even he had not foreseen how high the lake would rise that year.

Back on the water, Christopher identified yet another promising driftwood log that had to be tied to the stern and towed home for the ongoing garden beautification project. We also found a metal first aid kit floating in the water. I wagered a bet that the contents would be wet but I lost: the box was completely dry inside, filled with bandages and ointments of a very dated vintage. It was fun beachcombing at this time of year—no end of interesting things toppled off decks and docks in the spring storms, bobbed northward on the prevailing wind and floated into the Landing bay.

Monday, July 9

We kissed goodbye and Christopher drove off at seven a.m. in our car, "Mitzi." He carried along fewer tools than usual, a suitcase of smarter clothes for the big city, his passport and some food for the road.

While Christopher was gone I would concentrate on restoring my health and energy; the upsetting time with my mother had exhausted me. And I would make the most of the good weather—it had finally stopped raining after a month of deluges. I'd sit on the deck enjoying the view, putter in the garden, make comforting soups and read. Sympathetic and understanding, Lew McMillan gave me the week off from my part-time job.

I spent hours on the deck, moving my brown lounge chair from sunshine to shade, often placing it close to the far corner post where I could watch the lake. It felt like a ship's deck, wrapped around the south and west walls, surrounded by water. Like so much else about the house it was unfinished, with treacherous, rotting steps, no railing and faded paint, but it was a glorious place to sit, my ocean liner on the shore, with its colourful fringe of geraniums and herbs along the perimeter.

I was grateful to have this quiet time to reflect and rest before engaging with the normal routine again. Lying back in my lounge chair, feeling just a little self-indulgent when there was so much work to do in the garden, I watched the parent swallows at the nesting box under the eave beside the front door. It was the only local pair to have successfully hatched a family after the cold weather and torrential rains in June.

Back and forth they flew—making a long looping dive to the box, delivering a morsel of food and then swooping away, always taking the same route: across the deck, through the gap between the big fir and the cottonwood tree and out over the lake, gliding and twisting in the bright summer air with endless energy for their vital task. Watching them day after day I drew strength from their seeming confidence, their focus, their mission to complete the reproductive imperative. Their minds held no doubt or anxiety; they simply got on with the business at hand. I was comforted by their positive attitude as I grappled with the worries about my mother, and my guilt at leaving her in the nursing home.

In the late evening one parent (the male, I had decided) often perched on the topmost branch of a dead snag, his white breast flashing in the last rays of sunshine as he surveyed his domain and enjoyed a well-earned rest.

During that period Ozzie was constantly at my side. He was uncommonly attentive, so much so that I remarked to Christopher on the phone, "I don't know what's with Ozzie, he doesn't let me out of his sight." Normally he wasn't allowed outside the house in daylight, to protect birds from the great black hunter, but I relented, letting him join me on the deck, and he snuggled in my lap in the lounge chair, purring with delight.

Indoors I would look up, suddenly conscious of being watched, and he'd be gazing at me from across the room with his deep yellow-green eyes. I would tell him how beautiful he was and how much I loved him. Many childless adults live in this way, lavishing parental affection onto a pet. I called him my "furry son," and my "baby boy." He clearly adored both of us in his feline way. About nine years old, early middle age for a cat, he had trained his humans well, and everything was right in his world.

IN THE AFTERNOON I walked up the hill to visit Jillian Madill. The Madills had lived in the Landing since 1985, a retired couple quietly devoted to one another and to Tumbles, their cat. John, seventy-two, had retired seven years earlier from BC Hydro, and had worked at nearby Duncan Dam. Jillian and I had got to know one another while staining the cedar siding of our neighbours' house and outbuildings and had been friends for more than fifteen years. Hardly a week went by without a get-together for tea and a chat.

That sunny afternoon her open-plan perennial bed was a profusion of colour, a sea of blue delphiniums and campanula, pink and mauve columbine, yellow lilies, burgundy japonica, geraniums and scarlet bergamot. The raspberries were plumping out and beginning to blush pink; it would be a bountiful crop. We cruised the rows of vegetables and discussed the serious business of growing food: beans, potatoes, tomatoes, squash, onions and corn. Jillian's devotion and hard work had created a garden filled with hope and promise. The rain had been a boon, and now the hot sunshine was working its magic. I remarked on the box of purple petunias that cascaded down from the upstairs balcony, and the enormous pots of begonias and pansies beside the front door.

We sat as usual in the cozy dining nook off the kitchen, having tea and bikkies and swapping news. "How are all your house projects progressing?" Jillian asked.

"We hope to finish off the new roof as soon as Christopher gets back. It's taken three years but we're almost done, and Christopher's excited about laying the steel down. But then of course there's the bedroom and the deck to finish!" We laughed and shook our heads at the time it took some of us to bring projects to completion in this mellow place. It was a Kootenay thing.

The subject of elderly mothers was a bond between us. Jillian's mother was in far better health than my mother, leading an active, independent life in Kaslo. I related my agonies of guilt at abandoning my mother in the nursing home; Jillian assured me I'd done the right thing, the only thing I could have done in the circumstances. We watched a deer and her two fawns grazing in the shady meadow below the house, a scene of perfect pastoral bliss.

Back home, I emailed all the residents of Johnson's Landing, asking for a ride to town next day. I wanted to go to Kaslo to attend a meeting of our newly formed hospice society. This was an exciting development and I hoped to join the board. The care of the dying and bereaved was dear to my heart and I wanted to offer our new society whatever knowledge and experience I had.

In the past, a neighbour always offered to take me along when I didn't have a vehicle for some reason, but on this occasion there was complete silence. Apparently, nobody was driving to Kaslo that Tuesday morning—it was the first time in almost twenty years that I hadn't found a ride when I needed it! But I did receive a call from Jillian, offering to take me in on Thursday instead. Jillian liked to make Thursday her shopping day because Kaslo's health food grocery store received its fresh produce that day. She slightly disapproved of Christopher going off and leaving me for so long without a car, and wanted to help me out. I thanked her and we agreed to go to Kaslo together on Thursday morning.

I wrote to the hospice group and explained my predicament, but also admitted that it was hard for me to do much of anything just then, other than sleep, cry and try to make sense of what had happened to my mother, and my part in it. I found myself writing: "Perhaps there is a reason for the fates keeping me at home on Tuesday." Chelsea Van Koughnett, the leader of our hospice group, reassured me that all would be well; I should stay home and rest.

TUESDAY, JULY 10

In the morning I visited Kurt Boyer, our nearest neighbour, who was about to leave for Toronto to have a hernia operation. Kurt had lived in Johnson's Landing since 1971, and in 1974 bought his piece of land from Ruth Burt. He was self-contained, self-sufficient, almost never left the land and filled his time with mechanical projects, inventions, reading and his vegetable garden. He ventured to Kaslo or to Nelson, the nearest town, only when absolutely necessary, so this trip to Toronto was a major event.

He'd manufactured a new pair of shoes especially for the occasion. Raised in the tropics, Kurt had walked barefoot for his first twenty years and no commercial shoe or boot could accommodate his broad, splay-toed feet. He created his own personal lasts, formed rubber into sole moulds and affixed leather uppers with rivets. The results fit, and were pleasing to the eye, if a little unusual.

I took note of Kurt's instructions for watering the tomato plants in the greenhouse, then hugged him and wished him safe travels. I turned away and strolled down his untamed driveway, fringed with thimbleberry bushes, then crossed the road and took the shortcut path back to our house, about two hundred metres distant. It was extremely rare to have both Christopher and Kurt away at the same time and I felt just a little vulnerable. I was still so weary and found even simple tasks almost overwhelming.

The afternoon found me in my place on the lounger by the corner post when I noticed something odd. A coffee-coloured slick, a brown ribbon about half a metre wide, had suddenly appeared along the lakeshore, emanating from the mouth of Gar Creek. I slipped on my shoes, climbed gingerly down the precarious steps from the deck and hurried across the yard to the driveway bridge to inspect the creek. The water was the colour of a well-brewed tea. I looked upstream towards the mountain. What was happening up there? It wasn't unusual to see the creek run dirty at this time of the year, though I couldn't recall a change so abrupt and dramatic. But who knew? I probably wasn't thinking clearly.

Then the smell hit me—earthy, dank, with a tinge of something like pine disinfectant, wafting down the creek draw. Obviously the odour indicated broken and mashed pine trees up above us, but what else was going on? I recalled a similar smell back in February after an avalanche of snow brought tons of tree debris down the creek as far as Gerry Rogers's driveway, a kilometre or so upstream. But this stench was pungent, to the point of nauseating—odd and worrying. I squatted on the tiny bridge and watched the strange opaque water thundering underneath me. An osprey wheeled overhead, shrieking to its mate, but I barely heard it over the roar of the creek.

While I was in England Christopher had told me over the phone that it was raining non-stop. Obviously, I hadn't taken in the information, or considered what that much rain could mean, because I was so preoccupied with my own worries. When I arrived home on July 3, the weather turned sunny and temperatures soared to over thirty degrees Celsius. The heavier-than-usual snowpack was melting fast, which would explain, I thought, why the creek had been running so full. Now the water was this tea-brown colour and the smell made me shiver.

Gar Creek, where it crossed the property, was normally a tranquil stream that gurgled under the bridge, meandered between cedar trees and gushed over rocks slick with algae down the last few metres to the lake. The big old cedars along the bank suggested it was a well-established, mature creek that had been running undisturbed in its gravel channel for centuries.

The little wooden bridge in our driveway provided me an excellent vantage point. Various large boulders and old tree trunks in the creek served as measuring devices against which I could estimate the height of the water. One of my measurement boulders was now submerged and lost to view. An old cedar stump was only half visible. The wild black-currant bushes on the bank were being whipped and leaf-stripped by the torrent.

Wednesday, July 11

In the early light, after a night kept awake by the roaring water and the terrible dank-earth and pine smell, I stood on the bridge in my nightshirt and was shocked to see that the water was no longer tea-coloured, and no longer water. Thick chocolate mousse slurry was painting a mudpack on every leaf and twig, high up the bank.

I ran to the road above our house. Parallel to our driveway, the unpaved main road crossed Gar Creek for the third and last time and terminated a hundred metres farther on at the beach parking area and turnaround. Two culverts channelled the creek under the road. To my horror, the southerly culvert was about 70 percent blocked, while the northerly one ran at full capacity, disgorging a powerful jet that pounded against the bank.

The bank was beginning to erode. If it gave way, the contents of the creek would have a direct downhill route to our basement. Oh no, it didn't bear thinking about—our basement was jam-packed, filled to bursting with tools, books, two freezers, machinery, boxes of tiles, trim wood, our record collection, slides and photos, filing cabinets and all of Christopher's clothes in cedar chests and dresser drawers. I wouldn't know where to begin if everything was flooded with thick stinking liquid mud. My exhausted brain didn't want even to entertain this nightmare scenario.

At 6:30 a.m. everyone in the community received an email from Loran Godbe, who lived with his mother, Linda, and Gerry Rogers in the house highest up the mountain; he was our lookout perched on the hill. I remember thinking, "He's up early!" knowing that Loran was a night owl. But he hadn't gone to bed yet that morning. His words were troubling.

Hi All—

At 6:00 am this morning I heard a tremendous roar coming down the creek draw. I went running down our path to the creek, and got there in time to see a one to two-foot high (above the "normal" level of the creek these days) surge of chocolate-coloured water come past the community intake. After I got back to the house, I heard some more booming and roaring up the valley some-where, and as I write this, I can hear occasional boulders rolling in the creek up there.

When I was on our trail near the creek, I could not hear the roar of the coming surge over the normal creek noise until a couple of seconds before I saw it. I think the Gar Creek draw is a VERY DANGEROUS place to be for a while (few days). This also applies to our driveway where it crosses the creek. By the way, the washout on our drive-way is now too wide to safely jump across.

Be safe, Loran

Loran—contemplative and acutely observant of the nat-ural world—was our prophet, calling in the wilderness. He monitored the changes in Gar Creek as they occurred, and this was the first of two warnings he gave us by email. But, in the past, he'd sometimes speculated about hypothetical scenarios that hadn't transpired and I tended to take what he said with a pinch of salt. I persuaded myself that this trouble was something happening "up the hill," irrelevant to me. I closed his message and opened the next email.

The continued surges in the creek severed the emergency waterline from Moss Beard Spring on Gerry Rogers's land to the community's water distribution box across the creek, which supplied potable water to eighteen households on the south side of the Landing. This waterline was itself a temporary fix after the avalanche in February had wrecked and buried the permanent intake. The icy avalanche debris had not yet fully melted away. Local residents and several visitors were currently working on the waterlines in and out of the creek.

My sister-in-law, Renata Klassen, drove into the Landing mid-morning from where she now lived in Kaslo with Lennie, her elderly golden retriever cross, and provisions for a two-week stay in the post office cabin. This tiny dwelling, a treasured heritage landmark, had offered shelter to countless temporary residents over the years.

Renata, six years younger than Christopher, is a free-spirited woman who prefers not to be tied to one place. Where Christopher resembles their mother, Ren looks like Hanno, their father. She has his piercing blue eyes, a square jaw and a head of glorious, thick, copper-blonde hair.

Renata immediately remarked on the pungent smell from the creek. I took her up to the road above the house to show her the area of creek bank beside the culvert I was so worried about. We devised a plan, and Ren quickly collected two heaping wheelbarrow loads of gravel and some big rocks, and helped me improvise sandbags by filling a tarp with gravel and laying the sausage-like roll alongside the leaky bank. She had the physique for such tasks and I was encouraged by her presence and positive energy beside me. We anchored the gravel sausage with the rocks and stood back to admire our handiwork. It was a relief to have done something and I felt proud of our achievement. Such a tiny endeavour, but it was comforting and seemed to do the trick.

I'd made some vegetable soup and we had lunch together, also polishing off a big salad from the garden. Ozzie woke up and seemed delighted to see Ren as she grabbed him for a cuddle. Apart from Christopher and me, only Renata and Virginia (my mother-in-law) were permitted to take such liberties. Ren complimented me on my soup, then went down to the post office cabin to unpack and feed Lennie.

I spent my afternoon on the deck weaving a trellis to support Christopher's sweet pea plants. They stood four centimetres tall in smart new cedar planters, their delicate tendrils groping for support. Beaver-gnawed twigs from the beach became a triangular frame, and I wove a dream-catcher-like web inside with sinew. The task took several hours and I became stiff from squatting on the ground. Ozzie watched with interest from a deck chair, occasionally batting at the tail end of the sinew, but mostly content just observing the curious things that humans do with their time.

That night I was afraid. I lay in bed, sleepless and apprehensive, wishing Christopher were with me. The creek boomed under the bridge across the yard, its smell so oppressive I wondered if the house might already be inundated. At midnight I couldn't contain my worry, so I jumped out of bed and grabbed a flashlight to check the bank above the house. The gravel sausage seemed to be holding things together but the beam of light illuminated the thick gushing slurry that splattered the tarp and plastered every grass blade on the bank. I returned to bed and slept fitfully through the rest of the night.

THURSDAY, JULY 12

The day dawned as perfect a summer's day as you could wish for. The glass crystal that hung in the kitchen window sent rainbows of morning sunlight dancing over the walls and ceiling. A chipmunk scurried along the window ledge among

the leaves and tendrils of Virginia creeper that had smothered the east wall and gradually crept across the window-
pane. We hacked it back whenever it threatened to hide our
view behind leafy fingers of soft green light.

A longer email from Loran, sent in the early hours, described what he was observing in Gar Creek. My heart sank
as I read about the increasingly powerful surges in water volume. I wrote an email to everyone in the community describing my concern that the bank might give way under the
pressure from the one culvert that was channelling almost
all the water. I wrote, "I wonder if Highways could be persuaded to come out to clear the blocked culvert? It would
also prevent the road itself from washing out." Then I shut
my MacBook and hurried to get dressed because Jillian and
I were going to Kaslo.

I turned off the radio, then collected my purse, list and
shopping bags and set them by the front door. I ate a quick
breakfast and afterwards went to the garden to empty the
compost bucket and say goodbye to Renata; she was putting
things in jars, hanging up her clothes and settling into the
cabin. I cut some peonies and foxgloves and put them in a
vase on the mauve picnic table. We'd moved it onto the lawn
next to the cabin because the beach was underwater.

Renata told me she'd already taken Lennie for a long walk
beside the creek that morning. On the way back she threw
the tennis ball for him, trying not to send it down the ravine,
but of course it did roll over and Lennie plunged after it. He
had a struggle climbing back up the steep bank so Ren got
down on her hands and knees and pulled him up. He was
tired when they got back, and now lay snoozing on the cool
cabin floor.

Ren and I said goodbye, then at ten to nine I closed the
front door of our house and walked up the grassy path past
the water box and Ruth Burt's precious California redwood
tree, now more than four metres tall and growing fast. I took
a last look at our improvised sandbagging, wondering if it

would hold until I got back after lunch. Crossing the road I climbed the bank to our shortcut trail through a patch of birch and wild roses. The ground was loamy from years of leaf mulch, and was sprinkled with calypso orchids and tiny white queen's cup in spring. Now it was shady and dappled green with clumps of sphagnum moss. A varied thrush sang as I walked.

An ancient cedar tree stood at the top of the trail beside the road, its enormous hairy trunk the biggest landmark around. Owls roosted here, I knew from the piles of pellet droppings I saw on the ground in one particular spot. Kurt's driveway lay across the road from the big cedar and I took a moment to pop up to his greenhouse and check the tomato plants.

A few metres farther along the road, past the double cottonwood trees, and after the road made its second creek crossing, I took another shortcut up the steep bank, this time a dry and dusty path, barely shaded by sparse and straggling jack pines. Then I was on the road again, my route overlooking Gar Creek all the way up to Creek Corner. The formerly crystalline, delicate watercourse was a pounding, murky, stinking presence. It felt ominous, frightening, and I was beginning to loathe that earthy-pine smell.

I wondered what Jillian and John were making of the sudden change and was looking forward to meeting up with Jillian to talk about it. I hurried along thinking about Kaslo and our house there. Chores awaited, I knew. I could imagine what the grass looked like—I'd be up to my ears in things to do, certainly.

I was wearing a summer dress I didn't like for its dull checked pattern, selected only because it was sleeveless and cool cotton. I'd examined and rejected so many other more beautiful summer dresses. But I did put on two precious pieces of jewellery. One was a small jade bear necklace I'd given to my mother a few years before. She returned it because her arthritic fingers struggled with the clasp. And I wore my favourite pearl earrings: single pearls in gold settings, a gift from my mother on a trip to Gibraltar a decade earlier, shortly after my father died.

My purse contained my wallet and Canadian credit cards, my digital camera, my iPod and a small address book.

I left as one does on any morning. I didn't reach down to pet Ozzie, curled on the bed enjoying his usual morning nap. I didn't even think to say goodbye to Ozzie.

JILLIAN MET ME in her comfortable silver Buick with its grey leather seats as deep and soft as armchairs, and we commented on recent developments with the creek. Wednesday had been a frightening day for them too.

John had been one of the work crew attempting to reconnect the waterline above Gerry Rogers's driveway; John Madill and Val Webber were by tradition the residents who usually volunteered to take care of water system problems. John, Val and Gerry worked on the waterline, watched by Loran, neighbours Harvey Armstrong and John Lerbscher, plus John's son, daughter-in-law and baby grandson, and a visiting student garden worker, Aspen. The creek flow, dark and thick as chocolate syrup, fluctuated wildly.

As she drove, Jillian described what John had told her. "The work crew walked along an ice shelf next to the creek to get to and from the waterline. Gerry was on the ice shelf when Loran heard another surge coming and saw the water rise, pushing a pile of tree debris ahead of it. Loran yelled at the top of his lungs for Gerry to run, which he did, but fortunately there was nothing more behind the surge."

As they'd stood in the middle of the dark stinking torrent, struggling to reconnect the pipe, Val Webber had turned to Gerry and asked, "Are we safe?" Gerry, without a moment's hesitation, told him, "No!"

As we neared the Argenta Flats, two trucks passed us in the opposite direction, emblazoned with BC Hydro and Corix logos. My heart sank. I was fairly sure they were on their way to Johnson's Landing to install the dreaded smart meters. Many of us had been campaigning against and objecting vigorously to these electronic replacement meters, which broadcast information about our power usage in the form of electromagnetic waves. I'd pinned a notice beside our old analogue meter, refusing permission to replace it, but it would make no difference. I feared I was going to find a smart meter stuck on the side of the house when I returned.

Our drive was uneventful. We arrived in Kaslo at ten a.m. and went about our errands. House chores, indeed, awaited me—and as I expected, the yard in particular needed urgent attention. Uli Holtkamp from Argenta, one of my closest friends, had decided at the last minute to join me for lunch; I found his phone message on the answering machine, saying he'd be there just after noon. I set the table with a vase of flowers in the centre in anticipation of a delightful visit.

I extracted the ancient gas-powered lawn mower from the shed and by eleven thirty was struggling to mow the lawn, weeds mostly, shaggy and difficult to cut after all that rain in June. The mower clogged, almost stalled and I had to backtrack and repeat my mow-line. It was tedious and sweaty work.

Out of the corner of my eye I saw Andy Shadrack, our regional district's area director for the past eight years, waving at me. He looked uncharacteristically agitated, crossing the lawn towards me almost at a run. I shut off the mower as he approached. Christopher and I appreciated Andy's conscientiousness in representing and advocating for our diverse and opinionated local population.

Without any preamble, he broke the news. "There's been a serious mudslide in Johnson's Landing."

I gaped at him, sweat trickling down my face.

"Who lives at 2051 Johnson's Landing Road?"

I looked at the swath of grass I'd managed to mow and, frowning, swung my gaze back to Andy. "That's Kurt's house."

Andy's voice dropped to almost a whisper. "They say it's gone."

I began to shake. Lightheaded, I followed Andy back to his house, three doors up the street from ours. His partner, Gail, sat me down and handed me a cup of water. I sipped and talked aloud. "What an amazing stroke of luck that Kurt's in Toronto for the hernia surgery. My God, is it just— his house? How could that be possible?" Andy got busy on the phone, but information was hard to come by. I rose to leave and Gail hugged me. Andy signalled he'd let me know when he found out more.

I hurried back down the street, sweat drying on my body. I rinsed my face in the bathroom. *Kurt's house?* The phone rang: on the other end Renata sounded hysterical, close to tears. "I don't want to say anything unless you have some-body with you." Somewhere deep inside me, a cold hard loz-enge of knowledge sank and anchored. I already knew what she was about to say. I took a deep breath and tried to keep my voice even.

"It's okay, Ren. Andy already told me there's been a slide. What's happened?"

She hesitated and then blurted, "Your house is totally gone! It's just a pile of logs and mud!"

So Andy was misinformed—it wasn't Kurt's house, 2051, but ours, 2075. Ours! Of course! That made more sense. Kurt's house was above the bank, ours much closer to the creek. Ozzie sprang to mind, cozy on the bed. "And Ozzie? What about Ozzie?"

Renata had no news of Ozzie. I pulled the office chair over to the phone and cradled my damp head in my hand. Renata had more to tell me. Val Webber and his girls, Diana and Rachel, were buried in their house. The slide had also covered Petra Frehse's house. Renata described briefly her own miraculous escape, and urged me to stay in Kaslo. I hung up, bewildered. How could a slide down the creek reach Val's house so far away?

I could barely take in the details of how Renata had run to safety just before the landslide swept past her, missing the post office cabin by a few metres. Outside the Kaslo house nothing had changed, the sun was shining. Not knowing what else to do, I attacked the wretched lawn again until the mower ran out of gas. Ren's words hammered in my skull: "Your house is totally gone!" I couldn't grasp it or believe it. How could it be gone? Where had it gone? Where was Ozzie?

I went indoors and grabbed a glass of water. Just after noon it occurred to me that I had to tell Christopher. But what would I say? How could such an impossible thing be true, the house gone, the post cabin, only metres away, untouched? Houses don't just disappear. Was Renata right? Why hadn't anyone else called?

I phoned Eugene and spoke to Virginia. Christopher was out shopping, enjoying himself in the big city he loved. If it was true and the house was gone, he had to be told. I found myself speaking very slowly, enunciating every syllable. I told Virginia, "A terrible thing has happened. A landslide has destroyed our house. Make Christopher sit down before you tell him." She gasped and started asking questions, but I had to cut her off. I didn't know the answers and I couldn't talk any longer.

As I put down the phone, Jillian's Buick pulled up outside. I ran down the path, still in my sweaty work pants and ragged T-shirt. One look at her face told me she'd heard the news. After she received John's phone call at her mother's house, Jillian had driven all over Kaslo looking for me (I was at Andy Shadrack's at the time). She checked the grocery stores, then, on the spur of the moment, went into the insurance office, interrupting the manager with a customer. "Excuse me, but there's just been a landslide in Johnson's

Landing. My house is gone. Is it covered by our insurance?" The manager looked at her helplessly. Her reply etched itself into Jillian's brain: "She said, 'Now is not the time to talk about it.' And I knew immediately that we were *not* covered."

We stood together in the narrow band of shade under the eave at the back of the house. John was okay, but like Renata he had had a very close call. He'd given Jillian only sketchy details: the landslide had sideswiped their house; an enormous log went through it like a skewer, from front to back. Their cat, Tumbles, was missing. The glorious garden I had so admired three days before, the guesthouse, garage and vehicles were all gone. The fate of Petra Frehse, Val Webber and his daughters was unknown. I could not yet visualize what had happened. It made no sense that Val's house could have been touched. Easier to envisage how Petra's cabin, nestled near the ravine, would be affected.

Jillian was anxious to be with John, find Tumbles and assess the damage; she decided to drive back immediately. I would have to stay behind. If what people were saying was true, what alternative did I have?

I said the word "refugee" aloud.

In my pocket I found the deposit slip I'd been given at the credit union with the exact time of my transaction: "12 July 2012: 10:35:04." That had to be close to the moment the landslide began. Why hadn't I felt it in my bones? How could I have been oblivious to a personal and community-wide blow of such magnitude?

Uli arrived from Argenta just as Jillian was leaving. I waved goodbye to Jillian then threw my arms around him. "Did you hear what happened?" He shook his head.

"Everything's gone!" And I told him what I knew.

"That explains it," Uli said as we went inside. "Driving in I passed hordes of emergency vehicles with sirens blaring and lights flashing, racing up the lake. I had no idea where they were going or what it was all about."

I cried for the first time as he told me, "I *knew* I had to see you today. I had this weird, powerful voice inside telling me I must come." I looked at him and nodded. Uli and I have often had such inexplicable psychic connections, with one of us knowing instantly when the other one needs help. He went to the kitchen, got out the bread and found cheese in the fridge. "You have to eat something."

I had no appetite but chewed obediently. He held my hand. I looked at the clock. I couldn't understand anything. I swallowed. I chewed. It was such a comfort having Uli right there beside me. I'd left home at nine a.m. and now they said my home didn't exist anymore. I kept looking at the clock. It was now two p.m.

"Should we go and visit Ann?" Uli had brought flowers from his garden for our friend Ann MacNab, who was terminally ill and had recently moved into palliative care at the Victorian Hospital of Kaslo.

"Yes, you know something? I'd really like to do that." I hadn't seen Ann in several years but had heard how ill she now was. I stood up and went to change out of my work clothes. My hands were shaking and icy cold, despite the hot day, as I stripped and put on the ugly checked dress I'd worn that morning. I hated it, wanted to rip it to shreds, but I had nothing else to wear. I threw cold water on my face, got into Uli's green Jeep and we drove the half kilometre up the hill to the hospital.

Ann's room looked beautiful, filled with flowers and artwork, books and classical music CDs. Distracted for a moment, I gazed around with pleasure. I hadn't seen this room for five years. The idea of converting the old operating theatre into a new, purpose-designed palliative care room arose while I was hospice coordinator; we had raised funds and contributed ideas for its design and furnishing. Comfortable and inviting, it was like a normal room, with a hide-a-bed, armchairs, a stereo music system, a TV and a fully equipped kitchen area with a fridge and a microwave oven. Ann said she loved the feel of the room, its restfulness, the sunshine-yellow walls and blue trim, the paintings by local artist Pauline McGeorge and the bird feeder outside the window, rocking with activity under the ginkgo tree.

Ann was in the last stage of her long and illuminating life, serene and accepting, with an inner calm that surrounded her like an aura. A highly intelligent woman with three master's degrees—in Canadian literature, English literature and librarianship—she spoke with eloquence, wit and good humour. She looked frail and thin but was still very much herself. Taking both my hands in hers she gently held my gaze. "I am so sorry you have lost your home. It was a beautiful place. I knew it well, as you know. I used to visit Ruth there." This was no time for small talk. Everything we said felt significant, though in my dazed state I could remember almost nothing of our conversation afterwards. But in that moment it soothed me. Ann, who was dying, gave me a valuable gift that afternoon.

I said I would visit her again.

BACK AT THE house the shadows were lengthening, and the lawn-mowing remained unfinished. I spoke to Christopher on the phone and we talked about Ozzie. Might he still be alive? Was he trapped? Injured? It was agonizing not to know. Christopher planned to leave Eugene and drive through the night. The drive would take him around sixteen hours, allowing for a couple of breaks and brief naps.

At about five that afternoon, our long-time friends Bill Wells and Greg Utzig came by, just back from Johnson's Landing with photos and the first detailed eyewitness account. Bill had owned property in Johnson's Landing for many years; Greg and Donna still had a summer cabin along the shore from our place. Bill and Greg are soil scientists, intimately familiar with the mountainside above Johnson's Landing.

Bill told me, "We'd read Loran's emails and talked about them. His account of Gar Creek's behaviour rang alarm bells for both of us. The signs he was describing indicated something potentially very dangerous. That's why we went up there today." Greg drove from his home in Nelson and picked Bill up in Kaslo, about half an hour later than planned. "I was going to go straight down to your place first," Greg told me, "to return a tool I'd borrowed from Christopher. If we'd been on time, and been down there at your place..."

The mountain slid fifteen minutes before they arrived. They found the road cut off, and tree debris everywhere. "We were worried about your safety so the first thing we did was get down there and explore around your house," Greg said. "We found Renata sitting on the beach, very shaken, and she said you weren't home. We were so relieved." Greg explained that the landslide had slowed down, running out of material and momentum, by the time it hit the side of our house, folding it diagonally, and collapsing it. The slide had actually ground to a halt a few metres farther on, right at the shoreline.

I shook my head in amazement. "Good grief! If only it could have stopped a bit sooner."

They'd paddled Greg's canoe far enough out into the lake to see the whole hillside and sat there, aghast, gazing at the scene in front of them. Bill told me over a cup of tea how bewildered he'd been to see that the slide had jumped out of the creek and spread over the bench of land to the south. He'd noticed something else that troubled him, too: "Where's the water? Gar Creek's stopped flowing down in the slide path. We sat there for an hour but there was still no water and I'm worried about that. The question is, when is the creek going to start running again?" I tried to understand Bill's concern, but then Greg got out his camera and Uli and I were instantly taken by the images on the tiny screen.

Greg's photos showed how gently the house had shifted, not even dislodging the geraniums from the deck. Everything had collapsed but it was still recognizably our home. Windows had blown out, walls had flipped over and bits of furniture were visible inside. Greg showed me an atmospheric photo taken through a hole into the kitchen, where the roof now rested on the dining table. I felt a sudden burst of hope that Ozzie might still be alive. He could have found refuge in some nook or cranny, or crawled out through a broken window. I clutched at my vision, euphoric from the sudden surge of adrenalin.

Greg made me promise not to go climbing inside the house. He stressed the risk of further slides and I agreed to be sensible, but I'd already hatched a plan to go and search for Ozzie the next morning.

After Greg and Bill left, and while Uli cooked supper, I contacted several friends in Kaslo for help. I needed someone with a motorboat to take me to Johnson's Landing first thing in the morning. My friend Osa Thatcher crossed the front yard and I ran out to her, babbling about my idea. In typical Osa can-do fashion she volunteered to organize a boat and go with me.

Osa Thatcher and Paul Hunter are our oldest friends from the Landing. Christopher spent nine years helping to build their house. But in March 2007, Paul suffered a spinal cord injury, and he was now in a wheelchair, unable to live full-time in the Landing. They bought a house in Kaslo, just a block away from ours.

Other people were horrified when they heard about my planned boat trip and begged us not to go, but I was hell-bent and determined. Here was something practical and tangible I could do. I was going to hold my darling Ozzie again, and nuzzle my nose in his fur. None of the other losses would matter if he was safe.

Osa confirmed the details of our trip when she returned around eight p.m. with her friend Carole Summer, who brought me homeopathic remedies for grief, fear, shock and trauma. They said the house was gone, but was it really? I'd seen the pictures, yes, but I didn't believe it. Perhaps we could climb in and find Ozzie alive, salvage the valuables, extract some of the furniture. Perhaps all was not yet lost.

The roof and walls collapsed like a house of cards, crushing everything.

Chapter 2: In Limbo

The morning dawned overcast but calm. I'd worried the lake might be too rough for a boat trip. Osa had arranged with family friend Deane to take us over. I was up and dressed before six a.m., barely able to swallow a bit of toast and a cup of tea, anxious to be off. Every second counted, I figured, if my little Ozzie was still alive, terrified, perhaps injured. I indulged a brief fantasy in which I heard his voice calling from the wreckage as he ran towards me, his tail held high, indicating unbounded delight and relief that I'd come back for him.

Osa arrived on foot with their battered old beige cat carrier. It cheered me no end that she'd thought to bring it. Deane's truck pulled up. Uli, who'd stayed the night, waved us off in his batik sarong.

Deane is a skilled boat operator, calm and professional. At the Kaslo marina he went over the safety drill, handed us life-jackets and checked the boat, a sixteen-foot white fibreglass Bowrider runabout, with a 50 hp outboard motor.

"I was over twice yesterday," Deane said, zipping up his jacket and donning a knitted cap. "I brought Rachel Rozzoni, her three children and their dogs to Kaslo, then went back for the household essentials on the second trip."

It seemed to take forever to unmoor and putter out of the

bay at "Dead Slow" speed. It was getting close to 9:30 a.m. My heart was racing and I felt like screaming: "For God's sake, hurry up, come on, let's get out of here!"

Deane told us that RCMP and Kaslo Search and Rescue boats patrolled the shore. "I doubt they'll let us land today." I could tell he hoped that would be the case. Osa and I gave each other a look. We were definitely landing today.

Finally we were outside the bay and picked up speed. The wind tugged at my hair as the boat bounced over the waves, heading north across the great grey expanse of water under looming clouds. I soon got cold. I'd had so few clothes to choose from that morning and had made do with a pair of horrendous blue and white striped gardening pants, an old cotton tank top and a yellow work shirt that held no heat. Osa, well-prepared as always, handed me a windbreaker jacket.

It was nearing ten a.m. as we approached the Landing. A helicopter circled overhead but abruptly turned and sped up the hill. Had it seen something? The bay was empty except for one boat with a news camera. Osa said, "They've no right to be here filming people's misfortunes."

I nodded, thinking only about how I was going to rescue Ozzie. I knew he hated cat carriers. Would he be too frightened to let me pick him up?

We slowly cruised the shoreline. The boathouses, the canoes and other watercraft were already pulled high above the inundated beach. At the end of June Christopher had used the winch on George the pickup to drag the Burt boathouse three metres back because debris in the water was slamming into the front posts.

We continued round the bay. I saw Christopher's two sentinel driftwood trees, partners to our garden gateposts, standing next to our beach path. "Everything looks so normal!"

But what came next made us gasp: a rampart of logs stacked as high as a house sat at the mouth of Gar Creek.

Greg was right: the landslide had halted right there at the edge of the lake, and barely any debris floated around it.

The lakeshore itself was untouched except for the effects of the high water, which had covered many landmarks. I craned my neck to catch a first glimpse of our home through the underbrush. Where was it? "There!" I shouted.

"Oh my God!" cried Osa.

Pinned against the tall fir trees, the deck slanted downwards, the corner post snapped off. The walls were gone and the roof lay on a crushed tangle of cedar shakes, broken glass and deck furniture that included my lounger. The house stood only about ten metres back from the new high water line. I saw my planters and geranium pots, bright smudges of red and salmon pink, still clinging valiantly to the edge of the deck.

Deane cut the engine. "This isn't a good spot. It's dangerous and I don't want to let you off the boat."

I cajoled and insisted. "Deane, I just want five minutes to call Ozzie. Surely we haven't come all this way just to look at the house from the water?"

Osa chimed in. "Yes, we'll be okay. I really want to have a look too."

I gazed at the destruction in front of us. "It's been twenty-four hours since the landslide and everything's exactly the same as in Greg's photos yesterday. Go on, Deane. Surely five minutes on shore won't make any difference?"

He nosed the boat in, bow first, and I jumped out onto the rocks. Osa shimmied off and went racing away towards the house.

"Are you coming?" I asked him.

"No." He shook his head. "Listen, stay close to the boat. Tell her." He gestured in Osa's direction. "Stay close to the boat."

I nodded and placed the cat carrier on a log. I took one photograph of the weirdly deformed deck, put my camera away in my pocket and called out to Ozzie.

Just seconds later I heard an ear-splitting cracking noise above us. I thought of the sharp thunderclap you hear when a storm is directly overhead. I looked up: was this a thunderstorm? The snapping and cracking became more insistent. What was that deep roaring sound?

Deane shouted at us: "Run! Run! Run! Run! Run!"

I flew back to the boat, didn't notice the rough, uneven rocks. My feet didn't even get wet. Osa, however, had farther to go. From the boat I watched her scramble over logs, trip, recover, then she was at the shore. Deane already had the motor in reverse as Osa struggled to climb over the bow. Deane yelled at her to jump, and I hauled her in by her jacket, pulling on her upper arms.

For a split second that felt like eons the weight of the two of us in the bow held us pinned to the rocks. Trees just above the shoreline were beginning to bend towards us. The noise was deafening.

Osa screamed, "Go! Go! Go!" Deane was already revving hard and we were off the shore, thrusting backwards at full throttle as trees toppled. A mountainous surge of mud and debris thundered down over the spot where we had just been standing. The boat accelerated backwards.

As the mudslide hit the water it created an enormous disturbance that tossed us like a cork. Whole trees submerged and leapt skyward like torpedoes all around the boat. Any one of them could have capsized us. A tsunami-like wave, with log debris behind it, followed us out from shore, higher than the boat, catching up fast. It was right on the bow when it seemed to shrink slightly and gave Deane the opportunity he'd been looking for to turn the boat around, bow to the lake. Then the great swell hit us.

Deane gunned the engine into forward. Debris hit the propeller; the motor slammed left. Deane pulled back on the throttle, wrenched the wheel right and jammed the throttle forward again. We sped a hundred metres out before we stopped, the boat rocking wildly. Mud washed down the hill in wave after brown wave.

My eyes were glued to the place on the shore where we'd just been standing, now unrecognizable, as the creek disgorged its innards. The house disappeared under mud. There was no hope for Ozzie, or for salvaging anything. I stood up, grasping the rear seatback with frozen fingers as we rocked. The slide went on and on.

FRANCIS SILVAGGIO AND his cameraman, Mike, a Global News TV crew, were in the other boat and had filmed everything. I beckoned them over, urgently wanting to talk. Silvaggio interviewed me as we held the two boats together with our hands. This was the first of many media interviews I gave over the next seventy-two hours.

I felt calm and strangely clear-headed. I don't know where the words came from; they tumbled out. Fully formed sentences emerged containing concepts that struck me as surprisingly profound. Part of me was utterly detached from the interview and watched as—I was to see later—the stricken-faced woman with wind-blown hair in the ugly yellow shirt poured her heart out into the microphone. I told them why we'd come, my need to look for Ozzie.

Mike and Francis were in a state of shock themselves because five minutes before our arrival, they'd been walking over the slide debris, filming the devastation.

Osa's throat was so sore from screaming in fright on the shore she'd lost her voice. In response to one of Silvaggio's questions she managed to croak, "My house in the Landing was okay last night but I don't know how it's doing now."

After ten minutes we said goodbye and Deane turned the boat away from the mudslide that was still gushing down the hill. We headed back towards Kaslo. On the ride back I lost control of myself. I'd been perfectly calm and articulate talking to the reporter. Now I screamed, I cried, I shook till my teeth rattled. I howled because I had witnessed the reality: our place really was gone, swallowed whole. Ozzie really was dead.

As the boat came level with Shutty Bench, a community a few minutes north of Kaslo, I knew I needed to ask Chelsea Van Koughnett for help. Osa had her cellphone and, even in the midst of hysteria, I remembered the phone number. When we arrived at the Kaslo house, Chelsea and her husband, Ken, were waiting.

I lay down on Chelsea's massage table and she placed her hands on my head and gave me reiki, a soothing, calming treatment. I trembled at my core. Tears poured from the corners of my eyes, filling my ears, tickling my neck. I relived those seconds on the shore and the horrifying alternative: what if...? We'd cheated death by mere seconds. The anguish inside my head felt as massive, in its way, as the trauma suffered by our home and the landscape. What if we'd not made it back to the boat? Caught by the mud, I am trapped, dragged, smashed, beaten. And Osa lost too.

CHRISTOPHER, ON HIS way to Kaslo from Eugene, had driven through the night, stopping only for naps. He'd bought a cheap cellphone that worked until he crossed the border, and somewhere near Spokane I spoke to him. Still close to hysteria, I tried to describe what had happened. Christopher's voice was faint and far away, filled with pain and desolation.

He arrived in Kaslo at two p.m., looking years older than when I'd waved him off on Monday morning. But it was so good to see his lean figure jumping out of the car and coming towards me in his jazzy Amnesty International T-shirt, to see his caring face and mop of blond, sun-bleached hair. He told me how kind the officer at the Canadian border had been. "He asked me the routine question, 'Where do you live?' and it hit me: I had to tell him I wasn't sure anymore where I lived. We talked for quite a while; everyone there at the border seemed very shocked."

I remember our tight hug, his bony frame squeezed against me, his strong arms circling my back, his warm breath on my neck, and a dampness as we let go and cried. At least we had each other.

ULI'S PARTNER, SEÁN Hennessey, joined us from Argenta on Friday afternoon. He advised us to get lots of physical exercise to metabolize the adrenalin coursing through our bodies, and as soon as Christopher had recovered from the drive, Seán dispatched us on a brisk hike. It was good advice. Under broken cloud and sunshine, Christopher and I walked the Kaslo River Trail and sat a while at the viewpoint, watching the Kaslo River pounding below us in full flood. Glad and relieved to be safely together again, we talked, swapped thoughts, raised ideas and tried to make sense of it all.

A tiny part of me felt euphoric. We were alive! For just a little while, walking the trail with Christopher, everything seemed possible. We were free of all possessions! They'd been a burden, an albatross around our necks! All the old projects had been swept away, and a world of new opportunities lay before us! We could do anything we wanted…

The euphoria saw us through that afternoon. But when I curled up on the bed after our walk it was the wrong bed, and there was no Ozzie to feed, pet or talk to. There would be many tears.

SATURDAY, JULY 14

I dream I'm lying in the pink bathtub in our cave-like, cob-web-festooned bathroom in the Landing. In my dream it's Thursday morning, seven a.m., and I'm going to Kaslo with Jillian in a couple of hours. I love a morning bath and lie back dreamily, luxuriating in the hot steamy water, fragrant with lavender oil. My eye wanders over the cedar shakes that cover the walls. They are dark brown, random and characterful; they add a delicate scent to the room, and repel water from the shower, but if you brush against their rough edges you could catch a splinter. A length of string pinned across the wall above the counter displays my extensive earring collection, pair after pair, a line of silver and multi-coloured trinkets.

A pattern of ripples spreads across the bathwater. I glance through the open window, then shift my gaze to the bathtub and watch fascinated as the tiny wavelets fan outwards. I lift my foot then let it sink underwater again. Odd. I'm not causing these ripples, am I? No. The tub is vibrating. Now my whole body feels it. What on earth…? An earthquake? A surge of fear follows the thought. I hear a noise, an unearthly growling roar. The whole house shakes. I grab the sides of the bath, heave my torso upright, get my legs under me and leap from the tub, sloshing water over the floor. I yank my towel off the rail and flee.

Ozzie, on the bed in the living room, holds my gaze for a fleeting moment; our eyes lock. He breaks our eye contact and streaks for the stairs. When anything frightened him he always headed for his lair: a folded blanket on a high shelf in a back corner of the basement.

I throw the towel around my shoulders, dizzy, naked and dripping. What should I do? Front door? No time to get across the yard. I sense the "thing" as it rushes towards me down the creek. Instinct shrieks: *Get out of the house. Get out from under the roof!* Deck! I must get onto the deck. I yell Ozzie's name, beg him to come back upstairs.

It's hopeless.

Befuddled by the thundering din I run, trembling and clumsy. My wet feet slither on the kitchen floor and I almost fall. I pound across the kitchen, round the dining table, send a chair flying. I throw back the sliding patio door and fumble with the screen door behind it. The latch is clicked shut and I wrench at it in rising frenzy, ripping the screen. I emerge onto the deck and the booming, ear-splitting roar engulfs me. Sharp grit on the dirty deck floor bites into my bare feet. I dash to the far corner. I want to jump but falter at the edge; the deck's too high. I seize hold of the post and wrap my arms around it, my lifebelt, my buoy. The stinking wave of trees, boulders and mud crashes against the house...

I jerked awake from the nightmare with a yell and sat up, soaked in sweat. Thunder rumbled outside the bedroom window. Drum-beating rain pounded on the roof. Christopher rolled over and reached for me. Why was he here? Why was this bed so hard? Oh yes. Kaslo. We're in Kaslo. I fell back, convulsed by paroxysms of coughing. I could barely grab breaths between the harsh, gut-wrenching hacking.

I thought about Ozzie. His deep yellow eyes had shot me the message that he was terrified, regretful that everything had to end this way, and unutterably sad because this was our goodbye.

After my coughing fit eased Christopher and I lay entwined like spoons, his arm holding me close against his belly. I gazed out at the crack of grey daylight below the window blind and we listened to the rain. The sound frightened me. I asked him, "Sweetie? What are we going to do?"

He held me tighter. "I don't know, babe. I want to go up there and see it for myself."

"No! Oh no, please, you mustn't. I couldn't bear it if you were... At least wait until the rain stops." I turned to him and buried my face in his neck. He smelled so reassuring, uniquely completely himself. If anything happened to him, the last shred of meaning and purpose in my life would be gone. We held each other close for a few minutes, and Christopher agreed to hold off on his trip to the Landing for now.

Uli and Seán were up and moving around on the squeaky kitchen floor, making the everyday breakfast sounds of coffee grinding and toaster popping, punctuated by Seán's warm, chuckling laugh. Still coughing, I rolled out of bed and put on my dreadful check-pattern dress. One of these days I'd take great pleasure in burning the detestable thing.

THE RAIN SOON let up a bit and the morning brightened. The sky echoed to the beat of helicopter blades as rescue crews and media were ferried up the lake. CBC News reported that Vancouver's Heavy Urban Search and Rescue (HUSAR) task force was on the ground with heavy lifting equipment, assisting the rescue effort. But the weather was not cooperating. Violent thunderstorms in the early hours of Saturday had knocked out power lines and brought down trees on the Argenta–Johnson's Landing road.

I looked out on the grey, drizzly day; it matched my mood. I was cold and my chest felt constricted. My summer sandals were sodden and beginning to peel apart. I envied Christopher his suitcase of clothes and three pairs of shoes. And his passport! All my identity documents were lost, including my British and Canadian passports. I'd booked another flight to visit my mother, departing for London in mid-August. How would I manage that trip now?

Uli and Seán helped us prepare toast and eggs for breakfast, and Uli distracted me and made me laugh with stories of his chickens, ducks and geese at their homestead. After breakfast Uli and Seán left for appointments in Trail, two hours' drive away. Christopher sat down to call friends in the Landing. Most of the phone lines seemed to be working. As an experiment I dialed our number. It rang and rang, somewhere out there in the void. Obviously the line had been ripped out, but callers were going to wonder why the answer machine didn't pick up. I imagined our big telephone/fax machine encased in mud, swept rudely off the beautiful curved and varnished wooden shelf Christopher had recently built for it beside the chimney.

I left Christopher to his phone calls and went out bare-headed, scuffling along in my broken sandals, to see if the thrift store, beside the Mohawk gas station, might enlarge my wardrobe. Honora Cooper, president of the hospital auxiliary society that runs the thrift store, greeted me warmly in their tiny brick building. She'd already instructed her volunteers to let the "Johnson's Landing refugees" take anything we needed, free of charge. I gratefully grabbed a bright blue rain jacket, pants, a black wool sweater and a white shirt. But footwear would be more difficult. Second-hand shoes usually felt wrong, and anyway, the store had nothing remotely suitable that day.

In the street outside the thrift store, three local women stood in a huddle, deep in conversation, raincoats dripping, umbrellas up. They recognized me, put down their umbrellas in order to hug me, and asked how I was doing and what Christopher and I needed. I gazed at the kindly faces and didn't know what to say. What did we need? Well… just about everything. Every time I tried to grapple with this subject I was overwhelmed and went blank. I could barely string words together. But some needs were mundane and immediate and I was able to reel off a few of them: toiletries, a hairbrush and comb, tweezers and a magnifying mirror, moisturizing face cream. And shoes.

The Red Cross had set up its headquarters a couple of blocks from our house, in the Kaslo Seniors' Hall on Fourth Street. I crossed the road from the thrift store in my new rain jacket and poked my head round the door. Jillian and John were waiting to be interviewed. I went in and embraced them. John's face was ashen. I badly wanted to ask him about his escape, but he looked fragile and I didn't like to raise the subject just then.

Jillian looked exhausted but resolute. Like me she was in the same clothes she'd been wearing three days ago. Her grim expression told me they were going to do their damnedest to get through this nightmare. They'd stayed two nights with our friends Gail Spitler and Lynne Cannon in the Landing, and were off to stay in a Nelson hotel after lunch, while they used their emergency vouchers for clothes and provisions. Ann MacNab had got word to them from her palliative care bed in the hospital, to offer temporary accommodation in her house in Howser, north of Kootenay Lake. She and Jillian were old friends.

"How generous of her," I said. "Have you found Tumbles?"

Jillian shook her head. "They won't let us look for him. Too dangerous."

"What a worry for you," I said, thinking of my dream, and Ozzie's ominous and sorrowful countenance, feeling sorry I'd brought up the subject of cats.

AL, THE RED Cross team leader, was upbeat and welcoming, introduced me to their team of four, and offered coffee and cookies. He told me to come back with Christopher for an interview. Meanwhile I should write down our immediate needs on the flip chart next to his desk. I wrote: "size nine women's trainers, orthopaedic pillow, small backpack, MacBook computer to borrow," followed by our names, phone number and address.

I noticed that our Landing neighbours Colleen O'Brien and Patrick Steiner had listed diapers and other baby needs. This information told me they'd evacuated from Kootenay Joe Farm with their three-week-old baby son, Maël. Colleen's parents, Patrick and Carol, must be here too: they'd arrived in the Landing on Tuesday, elated to meet their first grandchild. I wondered where they were staying, and what Patrick and Colleen were doing about the farm animals left behind in the Landing. Too exhausted to enquire, I drifted out of the seniors' hall, enveloped in a mental fog. Osa would know where they were.

I wandered back to the house, damp, shivery and decidedly unwell. I'd had a slight cough ever since I got back from

England but thought nothing of it. Since the boat trip it was much worse; my chest felt gripped as though by a tight band of metal. I couldn't remember anything quite like it. I felt almost frightened as I walked along, gasping for air between coughing fits.

As I reached our yard two cars drew up. I opened the front door and shouted up the stairs to alert Christopher, then greeted Linda Portman and Maggie Crowe, who introduced themselves as local volunteers working on behalf of the provincial Emergency Social Services (ESS) program. They would be providing us with vouchers for basic supplies. I didn't know Linda, but Maggie was a former, long-time resident of Johnson's Landing. She gave me one of her powerful bear hugs. Maggie's a lady of substance, tall and broad, and I felt reassured by her solid embrace.

Michelle Mungall, our provincial Member of the Legislative Assembly (MLA), and her partner, Zak, got out of the second car. Young, attractive and dynamic, Michelle introduced herself, commiserated with us and requested permission to join our meeting to help her assess how BC's emergency response service functioned in practice. I welcomed everybody, and the four visitors and I hurried indoors out of the rain, depositing a sodden pile of boots, shoes and dripping jackets in the entranceway. We searched out extra chairs so everyone could sit around the dining room table. I sat between Michelle and Zak. The doorbell rang. Colleen O'Brien's father, Patrick, had seen the entourage arrive and asked if he might join us, on behalf of his daughter and son-in-law, as he had a few questions.

Christopher and I were hungry for news. Linda told us briefly about Thursday. She'd been stationed at the community hall on the south side of the Landing in the afternoon, assisting residents who wanted to evacuate. There was no power, and the hall had no phone; it was hot and uncomfortable, and it took several hours to come up with an evacuation plan. She'd driven back on Friday with Maggie, this time using Gail Spitler and Lynne Cannon's home north of the landslide area, as it was a much more comfortable place to base their reception centre.

Linda, clearly exhausted, had dark lines under her eyes. She explained she'd been called on to lead the ESS response because the chief emergency coordinator was away. What irony! After years preparing for an emergency, when a natural disaster of unprecedented proportions hits the West Kootenay, the lead person misses it. The rest of the team looked as if they'd been thrown in the deep end.

Linda and Maggie took their time filling out the ESS forms (in triplicate), worrying whether they'd completed them correctly. We made sympathetic noises; the ladies seemed a little overwhelmed by their task and in need of encouragement. Maggie slid the paperwork over to me. I tried to concentrate on the intimidating sheaf of forms and instructions, then gave up and let the conversation wash over me, hoping Christopher was taking in the information. I wished there were a simpler way: perhaps a credit card topped up with a designated amount of cash we could use where and when we needed.

I looked blankly at the vouchers. We'd picked Walmart— it had the most complete stock of clothing in Nelson—($150 each); a second Walmart voucher ($50 each) for incidentals like toiletries, medications and pet food (how I wished we still had pet food requirements). A third voucher ($315) would get us groceries from the largest Kaslo grocery store; and the last would provide a tank of gas for the car, from the Mohawk gas station. All of the vouchers would expire in three days' time. I noted various instructions underlined in bold type, admonishing us that "This is not a wardrobe replacement," and "Tobacco products and alcohol are not included." Pity about that. A small glass of whisky would have been a fine thing.

Overcome by another coughing fit, I wondered how on earth we'd cope with all these tasks. A mix of confusion and gratitude washed over me as I tried to take everything in. I was behaving like a zombie, but certainly had no wish to seem unappreciative. It was wonderful that the government offered this kind of immediate assistance. Disaster victims in so many other countries could only dream of receiving help like this.

Patrick O'Brien asked about the prospects of extracting their truck and camper, which were stuck in the Landing on the south side of the slide. All the belongings they'd brought from their home in Mission, BC, were in the camper. They wanted it in Kaslo, so they could stay close to Colleen, Patrick and baby Maël. Was there any plan for getting vehicles out? Linda and Maggie didn't know.

The meeting broke up. After Linda and Maggie left I asked Patrick where the family was staying. "We're just five doors away from you, in a rental house for one week. The Red Cross managed to find us a place, but it's difficult at the height of tourist season. Kaslo's full, and now there's all the media needing accommodations too." He went on, "The baby's not feeding well; he's still losing weight and Colleen's worried. No one's getting enough sleep."

I said I'd come by sometime soon. Colleen and her husband, Patrick, our newest neighbours in the Landing, were young farmers just beginning to establish their farm on the stony mountainside, and their heritage seed business, Stellar Seeds. Now they also grappled with parenthood and all the worries of a first baby, still so tiny. I knew they were a resilient pair, endowed with the boundless energy and optimism of youth, but even so, what a blow it must have been to be wrenched from their home.

Zak and Michelle were the last to leave. Zak took me aside and asked about my cough. I told him the truth. "It's been getting worse, and I'm finding it hard to breathe when I can't stop coughing." Zak told me he was a nurse practitioner and asked if he might thump my back. I readily agreed and he conducted a brief examination beside the dining room table. His diagnosis was that I possibly had pneumonia, adding "If you like, I'll write you a prescription for antibiotics that you can pick up from the Kaslo pharmacy." I'd never had pneumonia in my life. And I was amazed by the kind assistance, right in my home, tailor-made, when I needed it. I nodded, thanked Zak profusely and bent over a chair, wracked by another coughing fit.

After Zak and Michelle left, Christopher and I decided it was time we had our talk with the Red Cross and wandered over to the seniors' hall. Al called out a greeting and introduced us to one of his volunteers, Nicholas Albright, who led us to a quiet room next door in the government building for our interview. Nicholas was like his name: bright, cheerful and positive. He spoke slowly and clearly, perhaps aware that traumatized people have short-term memory problems, and struggle to absorb information. He was originally from Birmingham; I was comforted by his English accent.

We must have looked dazed, sitting there in the empty office. I was usually the talkative one, but neither of us knew what to say. Nicholas understood, smiled warmly and, after learning Christopher's line of work, suggested he might need a new pair of workboots. He was right. Of course! Christopher's were gone. He has large, wide, difficult feet; new boots were always hard to fit, and they'd be expensive. In the state we were in I doubt we'd have thought of such a thing ourselves. Our unfolding list of needs was so extensive we couldn't begin to identify individual items.

Nicholas asked if we needed new eyeglasses—another brilliant idea. He quickly phoned the shoe shop and the optician in Nelson and provided us with Red Cross payment vouchers. I folded the vouchers and tucked them away in my purse with the ESS vouchers. Nicholas also offered to keep Christopher's file open for longer-term assistance to replace essential tools. We shook hands, grateful, tearful and exhausted. I'd never imagined being on the receiving end of Red Cross aid. I blinked back tears. "I thought the Red

Cross only operated in other countries, responding to war, famine, national emergencies and disasters." Nicholas smiled and replied, "Oh we have work here too. Mostly house fires in this part of the world. And natural disasters can happen anywhere, as you've just discovered."

Christopher and I thanked him again as we left. We urgently needed to go home for a nap. The rain had stopped and the sun burst through the clouds. The streets steamed, and we peeled off layers of clothing and tied them round our waists as we walked the three blocks back home. How bright everything suddenly looked, freshly washed by the storms.

Our yellow and green house was cheery in the sunshine. The screen door stood slightly ajar. Between the screen door and the front door someone had propped a foam orthopaedic pillow. A black backpack hung on the doorknob, and a pair of size nine women's trainers, wrapped in a grocery bag, sat beside the step. There were no notes to say who'd left them. Inside, I sat on the stairs bemused, thinking of the Biblical adage: "Ask and you shall receive." The trainers fit perfectly. A message on the answering machine informed me that Randy Morse, a neighbour nearby, had an Apple laptop ready for me to borrow.

This was great news. Christopher headed for the bedroom and passed out within a few seconds. I longed to join him, but I urgently wanted that computer. I put off my nap and hurried up the street to Randy and Janet's house, five minutes' walk away. Randy brought out a silver case, badly scuffed and worn, with an impressive ding crumpling its lid. He laughed as he explained, "This old laptop has history. I accidentally dropped it over a cliff in the Himalayas, but it still works, at least for basic stuff like email."

Accepting Randy's loaner laptop with gratitude, I wondered what my own white MacBook, "Macaroon" as I called it, looked like now. I felt a twinge of horror at the thought of it, every orifice impacted by mud. It was ridiculous to feel a kinship with such things, but Macaroon had been my trusty servant in all matters technological, the holder of my addresses, memoirs, manuscripts, favourite websites; it remembered all my usernames and passwords. I had no idea how I'd piece together my world without it.

Back home, with the stuttering thumping of helicopters overhead, I plugged in Randy's laptop and composed my first post-landslide email message, intended for family and friends around the world.

Dear ones,

I am using a borrowed laptop. Cannot really think straight. I twice escaped with my life only by a miracle in the past 48 hours. Thursday morning an enormous landslide took out much of Johnson's Landing. It crushed our house and killed our cat. If I had been in the house I would have died. I was in Kaslo with a neighbour, whose house was also destroyed. Four other neighbours are missing.

I returned by boat Friday morning. Another slide came down and I only just made it back to the boat. There is nothing left. We have lost everything. We are in shock. People are kind. We have our Kaslo house but so much of value is gone. I have not told my mother, as in her precarious mental state it is better not to worry her.

You can see what happened by googling "Johnson's Landing Slide." I am interviewed in one clip. Please pray for us. We are devastated.

Much love, Mandy

Nobody was going to believe me—I barely believed it myself. Searching my webmail I found only a few names to send the email to; I hadn't bothered to upload my contacts and I couldn't email many other important people until I tracked down their addresses. Randy's computer felt wrong, unfamiliar and clunky under my fingers. It held none of my information. It quit Safari when I tried to search for news online. Writing one email had been like trying to walk with my legs hobbled.

I flipped the lid closed.

My mind was a closet, packed tight with a mental inventory of things we'd lost; it was a deep closet. As I moved through the house, tidying up, washing cups, feeling the newness of shoes that weren't in shreds, but weren't new either, periodically the closet door opened just a crack and I'd remember something. A knife-blade of grief leapt out and stabbed me in the heart. I suppose we define ourselves through the things we choose to share our lives with, though I hadn't made the connection so obviously before. Our possessions must give us so much of our identity and status. Without the familiar objects, paintings, books—without my "things"—I didn't know where to land or even settle.

A button had fallen off Christopher's shirt that morning and I didn't have a needle and thread to sew it back on. I remembered my delicately woven work basket, containing sewing, embroidery and darning equipment, sharp scissors, thimbles and a measuring tape. As for my knitting supplies and yarn, and the knitted jacket project I'd laid out on the couch to admire, so nearly complete... I inhaled sharply and slammed the memory closet shut again.

I found Christopher splayed out on the bed, deeply asleep. His careworn face, even in repose, was etched with lines of exhaustion and sadness. I joined him; what a relief to sink into oblivion and escape for just a few minutes—until the phone in the study rang and woke me up. The voice on the line was gentle and polite. Megan Cole from the *Nelson Star* newspaper asked if I'd be willing to give her an interview. I said yes.

Telling my story seemed to sink a deepening groove of belief into my brain. Victims of sudden trauma need to tell their stories over and over again, I knew this from my work with the hospice. By retelling their story, victims slowly convince themselves: "This really did happen. I am not making it up!" As Megan quietly probed with her questions, words flowed out of me. As when I was interviewed by Francis Silvaggio the previous day on the boat—I could hardly believe it had been only *yesterday*—I felt like I was at a distance, observing myself as I spoke: "You never imagine that today marks the end of so much you knew and held dear. When I closed our front door on Thursday morning, a chapter of my life also closed. And now, when I think back to the time before Thursday, it's like looking through a window onto a past world that ended long, long ago."

I told Megan how extremely fortunate we'd all been. Me, out of the house an hour and a half before it was destroyed. And yesterday, Friday, having just enough time to get back to the boat. If Deane had beached the boat sideways to the shore we couldn't have launched in time. If I'd heard even the suggestion of Ozzie's voice in the wreckage, I'd have hesitated, not left, and that would have been the end of me. If we'd arrived five minutes earlier, or if the second slide had come down five minutes later, I'd have been too far away from the boat. The temptation to climb up onto our deck was irresistible. If Christopher and Kurt hadn't been at a safe distance in Eugene and Toronto, they'd have been climbing into the wreckage themselves, right then, trying to salvage things.

If. If. If.

WHEN THE INTERVIEW was over, I rejoined Christopher, who was just opening his eyes, and snuggled down next to him. "What did you find out on the phone this morning? Who did you talk to?"

"Gail. She and Lynne are in the thick of it there on Rogers Road. Every journalist who lands in a helicopter sees their house and knocks on the door for an interview." I was glad that our friends Gail and Lynne were handling the media. I couldn't think of better people to put out the story. They would stay calm and be meticulously accurate.

"And the RCMP has it all wrong. They keep saying Petra was in the Webbers' house having breakfast with Val and the girls on Thursday."

"Well, we know that's impossible." Petra and Val had a romantic relationship; everyone in the Landing knew about it, and we also knew that Val's daughters weren't too happy about the situation, and weren't on friendly terms with Petra. It was ridiculous to suppose they'd have invited her over for breakfast.

"What else did you hear?"

"Apparently there's over a hundred people out there digging." I glanced at him. Christopher had the look of a man who wished he could be out there digging too.

The phone rang again, but I let it go to the answering machine. A hundred rescue and recovery people. Three times the population of the Landing: what an invasion!

Christopher rolled onto his side. "What do you miss most, at the moment? Apart from Ozzie, of course."

I took a deep breath and closed my eyes, stroking his hand. "I miss the silence. I miss the deep green shade from the tall firs that made the house so comfortable in the summer. I miss swimming naked in the lake. I miss the sparkling light reflecting off the water mid-afternoon, that danced across the ceiling."

We sighed deeply, lost in the vision. The yearning was a physical ache.

OSA CAME OVER after tea and the three of us stood together in the front yard, now bathed in late afternoon sunshine. It helped to have members of our Johnson's Landing "family" so close by, especially Osa and Paul, after everything we'd been through together; they understood our loss.

"Our place feels like Grand Central Station; the phone ringing, people stopping by," she said. She was inundated with food, and was driving all over town delivering food parcels to evacuees. Rachel Rozzoni, now in Shutty Bench with her three children, was missing her garden. "She was ecstatic when I brought fresh organic vegetables." We nodded. Johnson's Landing always had bountiful gardens.

Osa turned to leave, then added, "Oh. There's a plan to float the trapped vehicles across the lake on a barge." She went on to explain. Derek and Camille Baker had a barge, and Derek was primed to make the first crossing the next morning. Christopher perked up at this news: "I'm in." Renata's car was one of the vehicles stranded at the parking area by the beach.

I sat down on the front doorstep, my heart racing. The mere idea of going to the Landing had me clammy-fisted with fear. "I'd love to help too," I added—the Landing, to me, had become a life-threatening place, an ogre that might eat you up—"but I can't go."

Christopher told Osa he'd contact Renata and they'd drive out to the Landing in the morning.

IN THE EVENING, Uli and Seán returned from Trail with bags full of groceries from Ferraro Foods, the Italian supermarket: pasta, rice, bread, potatoes; fresh produce and treats—olives, special cheeses, chocolates and cookies. They stacked the groceries in our empty pantry and fridge and, despite our entreaties, wouldn't allow us to pay for them.

Uli showed me three summer dresses he'd picked out for me at the Trail thrift store. They were flowing, summery, light and joyful: one was a sky blue Hawaiian print; one was black, splashed with large yellow hibiscus flowers; and the third was a simple, sleeveless little black dress—the kind of thing every woman needs. I was moved by his thoughtfulness, good taste and ingenuity. He also bought me a large suitcase with wheels, for the day I'd set out once more for England. Oh God, yes! That was another reminder: I'd lost my expensive scarlet Samsonite spinner suitcase! Those

things carried a lifetime warranty that declared them un-
breakable ("The luggage that airport baggage handlers take
on vacation!" the ads said). I wondered what mine looked
like now.

Admiring Uli's gifts, my memory closet cracked open and
I remembered something else. I grabbed a chair to steady
myself, sat down heavily and buried my head in my hands. I
choked, then groaned.

"What's wrong? What's the matter?"

I could barely utter the words, like lead weights in my
mouth.

"Mummy's jewellery. All of it. And mine. Gone. Under
the mud."

Christopher put his hand on my shoulder. I hadn't wanted
to leave my mother's jewellery behind in her unoccupied
house in London. Why would I leave it when I could look
after it? The items were few in number: a gold necklace, cultured pearls, a bracelet and two rings. My mother seldom
wore even her engagement ring, for fear of losing it. She'd
told me many times how glad she was that I would have
them after she was gone. I'd brought the cream-and-yellow
Chinese silk bag back to Canada with me—for safekeeping.
Ten days ago. How ironic! I'd also lost my own jewellery:
not only my large collection of earrings, but several precious
rings, necklaces and pendants in a red silk bag—mostly gifts
my mother had given me over the years.

Christopher squatted on the floor in front of me. "Where
did you keep the jewellery bags?"

I gazed up at the three concerned faces. "In the bottom
drawer of the beige filing cabinet." I looked at Uli. "It's a
normal two-drawer filing cabinet. It's in a corner of the bedroom."

"Steel?"

I turned back to Christopher. I knew what Uli was thinking. Steel was solid. Steel could survive. Maybe there was a
hope?

It was all too much. I left the men to finish putting away the groceries, undressed in the bedroom, my cough reminding me to take another antibiotic. I pulled down the window blind and climbed into bed without another word, unable to face a single minute more of this first day in limbo.

SUNDAY, JULY 15

Warnings. Portents. Omens. How did I miss them? There were so many—the creek colour, the smell, Loran's emails, even Ozzie's obsessive attentiveness. In retrospect the signs were very clear. How was I so oblivious? By Sunday morning I can't stand the stark bald truth any longer. Lying in bed, halfway between sleep and waking, I rewrite the story in my head.

In my new, improved version of events I telephone Jillian Thursday morning and ask her to drive down to pick me up from the house. I'm worried and want to take some things to Kaslo. I gently scoop sleepy Ozzie in a firm embrace and whisk him into his wicker cat basket before he knows what's happening. I buckle the leather straps and set the mewling box beside the front door.

I pack up my knitting project, and stow Macaroon in my backpack, alongside the satellite radio receiver, my most recent journals, a manuscript of my book project and a zip-lock bag containing my two passports, UK credit cards and cellphone. I open the lower drawer of the beige filing cabinet in the bedroom and lift out the two silk jewellery bags.

We load everything into Jillian's Buick and get out just in the nick of time.

My daydream dissolves. It's torture because no matter how much I yearn for my version to be the true story, in reality nothing will change the sequence of events. I'd had ample opportunity to take valuables to Kaslo, but my powers of denial had held firm and I'd blown the chance.

I hear Uli and Seán talking quietly in the kitchen, packing up their belongings and getting ready to return home. They're such stoic friends. During the last three days, whenever I wailed and cried and raged, Uli held me and led me gently but firmly towards accepting the new reality: "No, you'll never see the house again. Yes, Ozzie really is dead. Your old life in Johnson's Landing is over." At times his words seemed cruel. Yet how strong he had to be to withstand my anger. How grateful I was for his strength.

There was nothing for it but to get up and face the day.

I FOUND CHRISTOPHER in the kitchen, scooping almonds into a plastic bag, dressed in his usual uniform of T-shirt and jeans, anxious to get on the road. My heart sank. The weather was grey and drizzly again. I so wished he wouldn't go.

Uli and Seán said goodbye to us. Back in the kitchen after they pulled away, Christopher and I looked at one another. He and Ren were leaving for the Landing and nothing I could say would stop them.

I packed almond butter sandwiches, apples and crackers into a cooler, with two water bottles, while Christopher drove Mitzi round from the carport. At the doorstep, with the cooler in my hand, I saw Renata come walking up the street. I wasn't sure where she'd slept Saturday night. She looked pale and worn out, and spoke to me in rapid bursts, gesturing wildly, close to tears. We gazed at one another. Only three days ago we'd said goodbye beside the picnic table in the garden. Today we found ourselves inhabiting a different world.

I watched Christopher and Ren drive away and turn the corner towards the highway. I stood on the front path, my hair damp from the rain, resentful and tremulous, wishing I'd gone with them yet relieved I hadn't. A lot more rain had fallen in the forty-eight hours since the second slide. A total exclusion zone was in force, and the RCMP were saying it was dangerous and foolhardy to be in the area. Christopher and Ren would have to sneak through the roadblock and hike down the hillside. What if more earth slipped? Would I ever see them again?

I looked at my front door, a yellow painted wooden door with a black cast iron horseshoe door knocker at head height. Christopher and I were going to have to get used to this house. I stepped over the threshold and climbed the five steps to the main floor. The house was quirky, a 1970s museum piece. I'd always been fond of it, in a way. The ceilings glinted with gold sparkles; the wall-to-wall carpeting was a garish grass green. Beige shag carpet adorned the main bedroom floor, with two-tone green shag in the two smaller rooms.

The kitchen décor was navy blue and salmon pink, with an ancient rotary phone on the wall. The countertop was a tiny space with barely a square metre to work on. Our kitchen in the Landing had had ample proportions and fabulous views. We'd revelled in cooking marathons, working side by side to prepare both my savoury dishes and Christopher's cakes and desserts. The kitchen in our Kaslo house was certainly not up to the task.

The bathroom, in true 1970s style, boasted an avocado green bathroom suite, a patterned countertop, clunky chrome fittings and gold-veined white linoleum. Not a cedar shake in sight. No more splinters. No more cobwebs. No wood stove in this house: I'd joined the world of all-electric baseboard heating. I stood in the centre of the living room, stretched and opened my arms wide, embracing the space, trying it out as "home." Nothing. I felt nothing.

In the Landing, they were still searching for Val, Diana, Rachel and Petra. I grabbed my rain jacket and left the house. Perhaps I could get some news from the Red Cross office. On the way I walked into the Mohawk gas station. On the front pages of both the *Vancouver Sun* and the *Province*, Val Webber's kindly smiling face gazed out at me, his arm around Rachel, seventeen; it was an intensely moving

portrait of father and daughter. I picked up the two newspapers, leaned my elbows on the counter, buried my head
in my hands and cried. The young French-Canadian cashier
came around, embraced me and pulled up a rickety wooden
stool. I sat down, shaking and incoherent. Our neighbours
were missing, presumed dead.

I fumbled for my coin purse, put three toonies on the
counter, pocketed the change and folded the two front pages
inward to keep them dry. I dashed back down the muddy
alleyway to the house, detained halfway by another coughing fit. Inside, I dropped the papers on the stairs while I
wrenched off my wet trainers. The thick roll of newsprint
unfurled and Val's face smiled up at me again. Christopher
had loved the way Val used to chuckle conspiratorially, as if
at a shared secret joke. I slid the papers inside a desk drawer
in the study, out of sight.

I turned on my battered old English radio for the latest
news, fiddling with the antenna to get better reception. Johnson's Landing was still the first and only story. I was relieved
to hear official acknowledgement that Petra Frehse had *not*
been with the Webbers, and an active search was underway
at the site of her cabin. At last! But three days had elapsed:
what hope could there possibly be?

Petra's cabin was sheltered in a grassy hollow beside the
creek—it was an old log house dating from the 1930s, with
heavy dark beams and a red steel roof, and windows overlooking the untamed garden where deer and bears browsed.
Petra adored the wildlife, especially the bears. Her hobby
was making characterful white teddies—she called them her
"spirit bears." Each smiling bear wore a bracelet, amulet or
necklace of semi-precious stones and carried its own birth
certificate. Along the property line beside the road, life-sized
plywood bear silhouettes stood nailed to the fence. Each
brown figure bore a name and a painted necktie.

I put the kettle on and rummaged for an Earl Grey tea
bag in the yellow Twinings tea caddy in the pantry. Selecting

a large glass mug I poured boiling water over the tea bag and prodded it until the brew was a rich dark brown. I splashed in some milk and carried my mug to the tiny deck outside the kitchen door, beside the carport. I leaned on the railing and stared at our tall juniper tree beside the kitchen window.

We'd always called Petra and her late husband, Jürgen, "the Teddy Bear People." They loved their Canadian home so much that Jürgen, in his last weeks of life, expressed his wish to die here. They flew over from Germany in early December 2005, and Petra nursed Jürgen through his last days. He died in the middle of January, and Petra buried his ashes in the garden. She endured two tough years of mourning, then rallied. She and Val began to spend time together and a gentle romance developed. Petra had glowed with happiness.

I sipped my tea. The last time I saw Petra and Val I was puttering in the garden, the evening before the landslide. They drove down to the beach in Petra's red truck and parked at the turnaround. I ducked out of sight, not wanting to intrude on their private time, and watched from behind the treeline at the shore. Val pulled his dark green wooden rowboat, the *Diana K*, to the water's edge and Petra stepped aboard. She looked radiant as always, her makeup perfect, her blonde hair immaculately arranged. Val pushed the boat out, settled himself on the polished wooden seat and, with slow steady strokes, rowed them over the still water, which glinted pink in the light of the setting sun.

RETURNING A LITTLE later from the stores on Front Street, I found a new collection of wonderful things beside the door, mostly anonymous. Living lettuces, their roots standing in yoghurt pots of water; homemade pesto; cookies; a bag of sweaters and shirts; fresh broccoli and tomatoes; a bottle of good French wine! I'd never been on the receiving end of so much spontaneous generosity.

Christopher drove up in the late afternoon. He looked slightly happier after a busy and productive day. He and Renata had cleared an area of tangled driftwood off the shore so that Derek Baker's barge could land. They'd transported Renata's car across the lake to Schroeder Creek, along with Patrick and Carol O'Brien's truck and camper, and several other vehicles. Derek was going to make more crossings on Monday.

I was impressed. "Isn't that typical! People get on and solve problems themselves."

"It would have been a long wait otherwise," Christopher agreed. "There are masses of people around, but everyone's focused on the rescue operation up the hill."

He handed me a plastic box containing a heap of small, muddy strawberries.

"I picked these in the garden, but the walkways are gone. The silt's deep and sticky; you sink right in. While I was picking them I met that journalist you talked to. Megan. She's nice. She had a TV crew with her. I didn't want them to film me but they did anyway."

Christopher, in his straw hat and backpack, appeared on the evening news, the collecting basket in his hand, as he gave reporter Emily Elias of CBC News one brief eloquent sentence: "It puts one's personal property into a new perspective."

Osa came to see us, and was glad to hear from Christopher that the barge operation had gone smoothly. She'd been on the phone for hours helping to coordinate the effort. She told us about a vigil in Vimy Park, organized by Rachel and Diana's young friends. I wanted to go but the first priority was a press conference scheduled for seven p.m. in the courtroom of the government building, three blocks away. HUSAR representatives would be present, along with the local search and rescue (SAR) leaders. I cooked up a pot of pasta and we had a quick supper.

INSIDE THE RED-BRICK building, the wood-panelled, high-ceilinged courtroom was packed with the public, the media and emergency response officials. We were lucky to find seats on two hard wooden chairs in a corner. A buzz of anticipation was palpable: the reporters sensed a substantial news development. We watched the circus in front of us as people untangled lines of cable, tested microphones, set up floodlights and focused their cameras.

Francis Silvaggio had bagged the best spot and sat cross-legged on the floor directly in front of the speakers' table. He jumped up to say hi, and enquired how we were doing. I introduced him to Christopher. Francis felt like an old friend; our encounter with the second slide was a bond between us.

The room quieted. Lisa Lapointe, the chief coroner of British Columbia, an attractive dark-haired young woman dressed in black, took her seat at the table, flanked by the commander of the HUSAR task force and various RCMP and Regional District of Central Kootenay (RDCK) officials. Without much preamble she announced the discovery of Val Webber's body, earlier that afternoon. The rescue had become a recovery mission, with Bob Stair, a forensic anthropology specialist and former coroner whose retirement home is in Kaslo, as incident commander. HUSAR would return to Vancouver, leaving twenty-four crew members behind to assist Bob. Despite budgetary constraints, the coroner's intention was to continue the search for Diana and Rachel Webber, and separately for Petra Frehse. Lapointe emphasized the continuing risk of further landslides, and her concern that efforts not endanger the recovery workers.

I put my arm round Christopher's shoulder as we took in the news. Val and Christopher had worked together on many community projects over the years. Just two months ago they'd helped re-roof the community hall, followed by another truly awful job: rodent-proofing and re-insulating the attic. I'd walked over to see what the two were doing and found them upstairs in the crawl space under the roof, wearing masks, lying awkwardly on their sides on the wooden floor, sweat drenching their coveralls. What a mess! Yet they'd laughed and joked at their predicament—it was one of the nastier jobs that had to be done.

And two days before the first slide I'd had a phone call from Val, needing Christopher's help to erect a scaffold inside the hall because he'd volunteered to install new ceiling fans. One more community project on his list.

We slipped out with our eyes down, hoping to avoid attention. But CBC Radio's correspondent for the Kootenays, Bob Keating, recognized me and asked for my reaction.

"Of course we'd hoped for a different outcome, but it's not a huge surprise after three days," I told him. "But very, very sad, nonetheless." I was running out of things to say to the media. My former eloquence had dried up.

The news of Val's death spread fast across the community of Kaslo. The discovery of Val's body meant that, realistically, there was no hope of finding the others alive. Christopher and I held this dark knowledge in our hearts as we slowly set off home, hand in hand. We detoured down to Vimy Park where, beside the lake, a crowd of mostly young people had gathered in a circle on the grass, many holding lighted candles. They were singing songs that Diana and Rachel had loved—Beatles songs. Almost all Rachel's grade eleven class seemed to be there, holding one another, crying and laughing, rocked by the emotional roller coaster of grief, still clinging to faint glimmers of hope—until someone quietly announced that Val's body had been found. The group fell silent into a moment of soft stillness.

MONDAY, JULY 16

A new week dawned with bright sunshine. I looked at the clock: already eight a.m. here, which meant it was mid-afternoon in the UK. I took a deep breath, gazed at the telephone receiver and braced myself. I hoped my crumbling mind was up for this challenge. After some delay, international directory enquiries located the number and I pressed the fifteen buttons in almost the right order. On my second attempt I was connected to Barclays Bank's customer service department, somewhere in the British Isles.

"No, I don't know my account number, sort code or bank address. It's your branch on the Isle of Man. I've been a Barclays customer for over thirty years.

"I can give you my full name, address and date of birth… Is that not sufficient?

"No, I cannot send you a certified copy of my passport. It's lying under several metres of mud! My home was destroyed in a landslide… Don't you understand what I'm trying to tell you? *I've lost everything!*"

The Scottish voice on the other end of the line sounded nonplussed at my evident distress but, no, she couldn't retrieve the account details on the basis of my full name, address and date of birth. The computer didn't store clients' information that way.

"Well it damn well should!" Tears welled up as I slammed down the receiver. How many Amanda Joy Baths born on that specific date, living in rural British Columbia, Canada, could possibly have accounts with Barclays' Isle of Man branch?

Christopher commiserated as I raged at the universe then collapsed onto a chair in defeat, wracked by another coughing fit. He made us a cup of tea. Slowly, while we talked, the tea, like warm balm, seeped into my brain and a few random neurons fired. I fumbled in the handbag I'd brought to Kaslo on Thursday. Yes! I still had my address book. I leafed through the pages and wanted to kiss each tiny ink entry. I had my bank details, both for my accounts and my mother's (of course her credit cards and chequebooks were also lost). I found another gift folded into the back flap of the book: a photocopy of my UK passport. I'd no idea when or why I'd put it there.

I phoned Barclays again and my magic numbers had the desired effect. This time the conversation gushed with silken obsequiousness. "I am so sorry to hear about your loss, Dr. Bath." "We'll have a replacement card and chequebook in the post today, Dr. Bath." "Is there anything else I can help you with, Dr. Bath?"

"Well... you might be so kind as to turn the clock back and let me go home again." No, I didn't say that. And I held my tongue when invited to "have a nice day."

The UK passport would have to wait till my next trip to England. At the top of my priority list now was a new Canadian passport. If my mother's health declined unexpectedly I had to be able to fly to England. Unfortunately I hadn't made a photocopy and had no record of the passport number. I contacted our federal Member of Parliament, Alex Atamanenko, and spoke to his assistant in the constituency office in Castlegar. I couldn't apply for a passport, she explained, until I replaced my proof of Canadian citizenship. Alex's assistant was clear and helpful. She would email the instructions, and advised me to fill in the form online, along with a second form to expedite the processing.

Randy's old laptop could cover my email needs, but internet browsing and online form-filling were beyond its capabilities. I ran down the block to Paul and Osa's house. The household was bustling with visitors and phone conversations. The open plan kitchen and living room smelled of freshly baked muffins. Paul was up and rolling in his power wheelchair. Jesse Howardson, who'd been working at Kootenay Joe Farm when the landslide happened, had evacuated to Kaslo on Friday and was staying in the basement suite with her friend Megan.

Paul set me up on their big-screen computer in the living room. He showed me some aerial film clips of the landslide that left me gasping and speechless. A wide, ugly brown scar had cut our community in half. The gash was huge and had spread out to the south, smothering much of the broad bench of land above the beach.

"Look at this." Paul clicked on a YouTube video link. There we were: I was in yellow, Osa in red, two small figures scrambling into a motorboat and backing off the shore as the second slide roared down the hillside. I watched it twice, shuddering at the memory, my stomach lurching in fear at how close we'd come to losing our lives.

I was usually good at filling out forms, but the Canadian Citzenship web page refused to cooperate, taunting me with rude red error messages. I gave up; it was all too hard. Hopeless! Jesse quietly took my seat and started tapping away while I threw myself on the sofa to vent my frustration and anger into the cushions. I hated the world, for its unreasonable demands; I hated everything. After several vain attempts Jesse concluded that the problem lay with the government website, not with us. She printed out the forms and gave them to me to fill in at home.

Over lunch, Christopher and I discussed our next steps. We came up with a perfectly reasonable plan, as we saw it: we'd take advantage of a Landing neighbour's kind offer of their summer cabin, move in and resume our working lives as though nothing had happened. Christopher drove up to look at the place. But when he returned that evening he shook his head. We paused, thought it through and realized our idea was yet another euphoria-fuelled fantasy.

The long-vacant cabin would need work. Neither of us could concentrate or think straight; we weren't in a fit state to simply pick up our employment where we'd left off. Christopher, a carpenter and handyman, had no tools. How could I go to work, then leave at the end of the day and *not* walk home across the hillside, as I'd done for the past eight years? It was impossible.

I phoned my doctor and she was adamant: because I was traumatized, I wasn't fit for work and nor should I even consider it. She wanted to see me about the pneumonia. I was taking the antibiotics Zak had prescribed, but still coughing hard. My doctor gave me the permission I needed to let go of my sense of duty, the obligation to keep calm and carry on—that so very British trait. I acknowledged that my brain was not working properly and I was often quite crazy in my thinking, hopelessly inefficient and emotional, unable to concentrate, and terrified to set foot in the Landing. Resigning from my job was yet another loss, but the decision brought some relief.

TUESDAY, JULY 17

Christopher and I floundered and struggled. The comforting familiarity of our synchronized life-dance together had been swept away and we hadn't yet learned the steps of a new dance. Inevitably, we occasionally crushed each other's toes and swayed precariously.

Our ESS emergency vouchers had been extended and we had until Wednesday to use them. We still felt diffident about venturing out into the larger world, however. Nelson isn't a big town, but to us it represented the city, and had many cross streets and small stores; the thought of working through the maze, and the hour-long drive each way, was daunting.

Disaster victims in remote, rural areas have different problems from disaster victims in the city. For one thing, it was inevitable that we would run into acquaintances. People would want details. I would happily have bought our necessities online.

However, on Tuesday morning we gritted our teeth and set out. The shopping trip was torture: a growing pile of painful realizations heaped one on top of another. We went into Home Hardware, scanned the shelves and saw reminder after reminder of possessions now lost. "*That's* gone! So's *that*. Damn it, I'd forgotten: we've lost *that too!*" Basic items of everyday life: kitchen knives, our brand new KitchenAid mixer, stainless steel saucepans and cake pans—each item thoughtfully acquired in the belief we'd never have to replace it in our lifetime. All gone. We stumbled out of the store without buying anything.

When we met people we tried to be convivial but the effort was exhausting. After a while we kept our heads down, avoided eye contact and masqueraded invisibility. I was easily made angry. In the optician's I overheard an acquaintance complaining that she'd driven all the way from Kaslo because they'd called her in, but her glasses were not in fact ready. I stood in a corner by the window with Christopher and a friend. I should have been ashamed of myself but I glared, and raged inwardly at the pettiness of this lady's worries. I felt like screaming, "You have *nothing* to complain about!"

My doctor decided I was suffering from pertussis—whooping cough—rather than pneumonia. Armed with my doctor's medical note and my record of employment, we drove down to the mall and, while Christopher looked in the bookstore, I sought assistance from the Service Canada government office. It was mid-afternoon and I was fading fast from fatigue. In a small voice I told the woman at the front desk why I was there. She came out and put her arms around me with tears in her eyes, then sat me down at the computer and personally guided me through the lengthy employment insurance application form.

In my experience, in times of intense emotional pain, we are acutely sensitive to human warmth and, conversely, to callousness. Kind gestures shored me up.

Driving out of Nelson we turned on the car radio and heard that the body of a young woman, found the previous day, had been confirmed as Diana Webber. We had nothing worthwhile to say. I watched the maple grove at Kokanee Creek Provincial Park flash past the window, the dappled sunlight glinting through its summer foliage. I thought about our friend Bob Stair, the coroner, and his team of helpers in the Landing, excavating through the sticky, muddy moonscape at the Webbers' house. What a terrible and sad task. I hoped Rachel's body lay nearby.

I remembered Diana in the role of Yenta the matchmaker in the 2007 school production of *Fiddler on the Roof*, with her best friends Lila Taylor and our niece Margie Smith in the roles of Tzeitel and Hodel, the first and second daughters. Margie, Lila and Diana were lifelong friends who grew up together in Johnson's Landing. We called them the Three Musketeers. And last summer I'd seen the three girls in Kaslo, looking like figures from a period drama, in floor-length floral summer dresses. They'd promenaded up the street from the park, giggling and chatting, looking utterly beautiful. Diana had extravagant, long black hair framing a pale, striking, unconventional face, alight with sharp intelligence. I couldn't believe she was gone.

By the end of Tuesday, back home, our nerves frayed, I jangled with adrenalin and couldn't stop talking. Christopher said he wished I would just *shut up!* He locked himself in the dank basement room. Shaken, I put things away and made a snack. He refused to come up for supper. I climbed into bed alone, wondering how much worse it could get.

WEDNESDAY, JULY 18

The next morning Christopher was upstairs. We kissed and made up, talked and cried together. We reminisced about the house; we would cherish the memories. We vowed to be gentle with each other.

But the process of sudden recollection and mourning was unrelenting. Christopher sat down next to my desk shortly after breakfast, his face stricken. "I've just realized: we've lost all the Christmas tree ornaments."

Within days of my email to family and friends around the world, the first airmail parcels and letters arrived. Clinique face cream, quadruple Belgian chocolate cookies, Marmite and strong black tea. Books. Money. My brother in Australia sent flowers. And still more gifts appeared regularly at our door. We were sustained by a multitude of caring neighbours and friends who held us in their hands, hearts and thoughts. I didn't know how to express my gratitude. Words seemed inadequate. Tears and hugs were sometimes my only vocabulary. Everyone seemed to understand.

We saw an ad in our weekly advertiser, *Pennywise*, for a Toyota RAV4, 1998 vintage. We'd yearned for a RAV, and now our need was even greater because we'd lost Christopher's beloved old Toyota Tercel, "Jerald." We quickly realized that this was a vehicle we knew, a friend's RAV4—not only was it the model we wanted, it was the very vehicle Christopher had long admired for its uplifting and unusually intense dark blue colour. He'd once called out to Elizabeth as she drove by, "I covet your car!"

We phoned, holding out little hope, but it was still available. It had over 300,000 kilometres on the clock, which had put people off. Elizabeth was sitting in the back seat as we returned from our test drive. We loved the car and said we'd buy it. In a quiet but firm voice she said, "No. I'm giving it to you." Stunned, we tried to negotiate at least a partial payment, but without success.

Next, out of the blue, came offers of new computers: a brand new MacBook Pro for me, and a reconditioned one for Christopher, paid for by a couple we knew only slightly, who lived north of Kaslo. The gifts and messages of encouragement helped renew our confidence in life.

Feeling both heartened and more in control of my destiny, I unpacked my new laptop and began to rebuild my cyber-life, networks, favourite websites and email contacts, tapping the details onto the smart, back-lit keyboard, feeding intelligence into its brain, making the computer my own.

What a miracle of modern genius these glorious machines are! Soon I began the first draft of a story describing what had happened to us. Writing was my escape.

When the new laptop was set up, Christopher downloaded the photos from his camera. Fortunately, they spanned all of 2012 because he hadn't deleted them from the camera's memory card. From winter snows through spring: apple blossoms in the front yard, lily of the valley beside the front door in May. There was only one photo of the house itself, taken on Sunday, July 8, the day before Christopher left for Eugene.

The photo showed the newly unloaded steel roofing, the sheets shiny, sharp-edged, forest green, poised and ready to be raised to the roof and screwed down. I was in the picture, too, a sunlit figure in white waving from the front door, honeysuckle in full bloom clambering up the pillar behind me. The Japanese maple tree was so tall, red and vibrant. And in the foreground stood the carport, repository of many precious things: Christopher's vintage Italian Moto Morini motorbike, his hand-built bicycle, his table saw and tools. And old Jerald, bronze and rusty, stood in front of the carport, a mobile tool chest for Christopher's jobs around the Landing.

Christopher and Renata had taken photos in June, on a canoe trip to the Argenta Flats. They laughed and made silly faces in selfie portraits. The day was sunny and breezy, the willows newly leafed out. Everything looked utterly beautiful and normal. And we imagined life would go on as it always had.

ONE WEEK AFTER the landslides, Rachel Webber and Petra Frehse were still unaccounted for and the search was called off. On Wednesday Lisa Lapointe informed the media that it was time to reassess the situation. "We need to step back now and consider our options in terms of recovery of the other two victims." Noting that the area remained unstable and very dangerous, the chief coroner praised the professionalism of those involved in the recovery, but warned that the two remaining victims might never be located in a debris field that measured thirty-four hectares.

The decision provoked an uproar of protest from some in the community. While Petra's cabin was deeply buried, Rachel probably lay close to the area where her father and sister had been found. Some of Rachel's young friends refused to accept the prospect of not recovering her. If the Coroners Service wouldn't do it they vowed to go to Johnson's Landing and dig with their own hands.

The last photo of our house shows the newly unloaded steel roofing standing ready to be raised to the roof. I am the figure waving from the front door, beside the honeysuckle in full bloom.

Chapter 3: Going Back

I PULLED UP the bedroom window blind and could hardly believe my eyes: a cloudless blue sky, promising the first really hot day since I'd left my other home. The day felt both propitious and significant—a whole week had passed and today I was going back to see the devastation for myself. Apprehensive but resolute, I was ready to accompany Christopher whatever happened. We'd defy the evacuation order and take our chances.

I got dressed: crisp new beige shorts from Walmart and a long-sleeved cotton shirt. I wished I had a wide-brimmed hat to protect my face from sunburn, but made do with a torn gardening hat I found in the back of the closet, better than nothing. I filled my new backpack with snacks, water, pasta salad for lunch and a pair of newly purchased rubber beach shoes, in case I had to wade through mud. I told myself that the risk of another slide had diminished and that everything would be okay.

Christopher loaded a garden shovel and a pick into the car.

"What are those for?"

"I'm going to see if I can dig into my storage shed. It's right at the edge of the slide, knocked flat, but I can see my chain saws and some bicycle parts underneath the wall. I'd love to get them out of there."

After a quick breakfast we set out in Mitzi. We drove

north and stopped at the viewpoint directly across the lake from the Landing. I buzzed with adrenalin, excitement and dread, as I scoured the landscape for familiar signs. Christopher handed me his binoculars. Down at our place I could just make out the clump of trees that had held firm as the waves of mud swept down on either side of them. A line of white water traced a downward path to the left of the trees: Gar Creek had cut itself a new channel on the north side of the house. The wide bench of land above the beach was a bald clear-cut, the soil streaked in varying shades of red, beige and brown. Peculiar. Unspeakably ugly. Menacing. And sad. Rachel and Petra still lay somewhere under there.

At the head of the lake we turned right onto the oh-so-familiar road that had always led us homeward. How many times had we puttered along this road in the past twenty years? Christopher steered on automatic pilot, intimately cognizant of every pothole, the deceptive bend with the slippery loose gravel, all the blind spots, crumbling shoulders, the treacherous places where rocks fell. Each perilous section had a name: Peek-a-boo Hill (nasty blind spot); Frigidaire Narrows (where the refrigerator-laden recycling truck had plunged to a watery grave); The Bluffs (where a fully loaded cement truck gallantly gave way to an oncoming car and sank into the soft outer shoulder, almost tipping over the vertical cliff); Schindlers' Hill (which we'd gently slid down backwards, traction-less, in the deep snows of our first winter in the Landing, later to be rescued and towed uphill by Bill Wells and his Land Cruiser).

A security roadblock erected at the top of the hill stopped traffic just beyond the turn to Rogers Road, but we turned left on Rogers and parked at the turnaround at the top. Gail and Lynne, two of our dearest friends, came down the driveway to meet us with Tinker, their dog, bounding and barking in excitement. I threw my arms around everyone, including the dog. I tried to say something appropriate to the occasion, tried to put into words how much it meant to me to see them all again, but instead burst into tears. I stepped aside, gesturing that I was okay, and struggled to compose myself.

While Christopher talked to Gail and Lynne and gave Tinker a full head and body rubdown, I walked around the side of their house, blowing my nose. Lynne's flower beds were immaculate. The lawn was deep green and freshly mowed. Birds, including countless hummingbirds, flitted and buzzed to and fro between the many feeders. The place felt peaceful, serene, and looked utterly unchanged.

I sat down at their circular cedar picnic table, in the shade of the large walnut tree, and gazed at the breathtaking view to the south. The meadow and apple orchards basked in sunshine, the lake stretched away beyond the trees. The mountain, Mount Tyrell, rose majestically above the dense, forested hillside. We'd always loved that mountain, and called it our mountain—a beloved landmark that we greeted every day through the kitchen window. Christopher had once scaled to its pointed peak, one summer long ago, with Paul and Osa.

Gail sat down next to me at the table and I turned to her, incredulous. "But everything looks exactly like it did... before! You'd never imagine anything bad or different lay beyond that line of trees."

Gail guffawed, but I'd learned that her laughter sometimes indicated discomfort rather than mirth. When she spoke her voice was hesitant and shook slightly. "Yes," she agreed. "Nothing has changed here—and everything has changed." We contemplated her words for a moment.

Gail said, "You know, it's strange. People think Lynne and I should be doing fine because the landslide didn't touch this property. But *we* weren't untouched. You are gone. Jillian and John are gone. Linda and Loran. Val, the girls, Petra... That's almost a third of this community—gone. We don't inhabit a bubble. The impact on all of us is huge."

She changed the subject. "I was on the phone to you, leaving a message on your answering machine, when the landslide came down, did you know that?"

I looked at her in surprise. "Really? What were you calling about?"

"About your email, the one where you described the blocked culvert, and your worry that the basement might flood."

"Oh yes, I remember now." I'd written that email a million years ago, in another world.

Gail went on. "I suggested you phone the Highways maintenance guys and tell them it's *their* culvert and they need to come and unblock it! But while I was talking the power went out and we heard a rumbling noise."

"Could you see it from here?"

"No. We saw dust rising out of the gulley, beyond those trees." I looked out to the treeline. The whole thing was unimaginable.

"So you didn't know I'd gone to Kaslo?"

She shook her head. "We didn't know for several hours where you were."

Lynne and Christopher joined us and we gladly accepted Lynne's offer of iced raspberry cordial. We'd often sat companionably together here in the shade of the walnut tree, remarking on local news and musing on the quirks of life. Our interests frequently meshed but our opinions sometimes didn't, which led to lively and stimulating debate as we threw controversial subjects into the air and picked them apart over tea or dinner.

I asked Lynne how she was doing. Tears welled up as she tried to describe those first few days. They'd gladly offered a sanctuary for Jillian, John and Renata. They'd received countless journalists, and provided bathroom facilities for the first rescue crews, before the arrival of the portable toilets. They'd hosted emergency medical responders, the ESS ladies and a delegation of the Red Cross. The helicopter traffic had been unrelenting, right up until yesterday when the search was called off and things had quieted down again.

I sipped my ice-cold cordial and watched the bees at work among the pastel snapdragons. How could everything here look so normal? I couldn't wrap my mind around it. Had nothing really happened after all? Lynne called my name and beckoned me indoors to look through a pile of clothes she'd pulled out of her closet. Several pairs of trousers and a couple of blouses fitted me perfectly. Our neighbour Eric Schindler had also made a clothing donation with John Madill and Christopher in mind. We called Christopher indoors to try things on. Being much the same size and build as Eric, he was able to pick out several jackets, shirts and trousers.

"Next time you come, we'll have books for you!" Lynne said, smiling. Gail and Lynne were bookworms whose magnificent library had to be 'culled' from time to time to make space for the new arrivals from Amazon. I thanked them warmly, but my memory closet gave me another jolt. We'd had hundreds, no, thousands of books—they were our passion too. Shelves upon shelves of them, in the living room, bedroom and basement. Beloved works of fiction, biography, history; favourite volumes by Spanish poets Antonio Machado and Federico García Lorca. Christopher had atlases, reference books, woodworking manuals, art books and architectural textbooks. Behind the couch we'd kept an entire shelf full of cookbooks, dog-eared, splashed with ingredients and carefully annotated. I shook myself: *No! I must not think about these things.*

We thanked Gail and Lynne for our clothing gifts, and for the pleasure of sitting in their glorious garden oasis. Tinker wagged her tail and watched, crestfallen, as we walked down the drive to the car. Christopher was a favourite friend of hers. Down at the roadblock we informed the security guard that we were just paying a visit to Roger and Carol a hundred metres farther on, and he waved us through. We'd already arranged to leave the car at their place and hike on down the hill.

Roger and Carol's property, like Gail and Lynne's, was untouched by any sign of the landslide. We parked, greeted our friends and stood together in the shade of a cedar tree. Roger, a rangy figure, his long hair tied back in a ponytail, told us about his lucky escape.

"I was down in the Gar Creek draw almost every day for the past month, helping Gerry Rogers clear avalanche debris off his driveway. I had my backhoe down there, lifting logs and cleaning up the icy, woody mess. But on the day before the landslide I suddenly felt spooked. The creek was running brown; the water smelt dank and earthy and was making sudden surges. I was afraid a big wave or flash flood could sweep me away—I wouldn't have heard it coming over the noise of the creek and my machine. So I drove the backhoe out on Wednesday afternoon and parked it on Kootenay Joe Road. Just in time, and well out of danger, as it turned out."

I looked at Carol. "What did you do when you heard the slide come down?"

Carol, small, wiry and athletic, gave me a warm smile and pointed through the garden fence at a freshly turned vegetable bed. "I was standing right there, in the garden, about to harvest my garlic crop. It sounded like a semi truck was coming down the driveway opposite, but it kept getting louder. After everything stopped I wondered if it was a flash flood from water dammed up behind the snow avalanche debris. I was worried about Roger so I jumped on my bicycle and tore down the road to Creek Corner, but couldn't get very far because trees and debris lay everywhere. I met Gail and Lynne in their car, and we wondered if you were all right. A bit later I saw Roger on the other side and we shouted across the divide that we were both okay. I realized this was a landslide and your house had to have been hit, so I dashed down the hill beside the creek as fast as I could. When I saw the building collapsed like that I clambered all over the wreckage, calling you. I was afraid you were still inside."

My heart was pounding. "What about the next day, and the second slide?"

"We were both here at home. We'd slept in, exhausted from running around on Thursday. We heard the second slide—it took more than an hour to flush out. After it was mostly over we walked down to Creek Corner and were amazed at how dramatically everything had changed. The incredible mess of tree debris was gone from the creek gulley. It was all scoured out and the gravel groomed flat. But you couldn't walk on it, and even now it's still quite soft in places, like quicksand. We used our kayaks to get around to the other side. But you should see the lake, it's full of tangled trees that flushed down, so it's really hard to launch the kayaks on and off the shore."

Christopher and I were anxious to get going. Roger and Carol joined us and we hiked the hillside trail down to Kurt's place, much closer to the creek. We found him outside his workshop, smiling broadly in welcome, looking remarkably relaxed and calm, his wild white hair and beard neatly trimmed. Christopher and I both put our arms round him and we held each other in a threesome embrace. "Kurt!" I said. "How are you feeling?"

"Never better," he replied with an ironic chuckle. "The surgery was a great success. I've got my energy back and the pain's completely gone."

I stepped back into the shade of his porch, trying to avoid the sun hitting my face. "I'm so sorry I couldn't water your tomato plants. I guess life kind of got in the way. When did you hear about it?"

Kurt eyed me thoughtfully. He seemed curiously serene. "I got the news, in Toronto, from Denise in Argenta. My immediate reaction was, 'Oh so *that's* what was going on.' Driving out on Wednesday morning I'd had a premonition that something strange was about to happen. I stopped at

Creek Corner and took several photos, but the place creeped me out and I felt quite uncomfortable standing there. So you might say I was prepared... sort of."

"Did you see any pictures while you were in the hospital?"

"Yes, the guy in the next bed showed me the news coverage on his computer. I was completely disorientated till I noticed Christopher's upended driftwood trees on the beach. Then I looked over to Ruth's house. I probably knew that house better than anyone; I did a lot of rebuilding on it over the years. There was no house standing there anymore, and *that* was a hard moment for me."

"And how's your place doing?"

"Well, everything's intact except for that gaping moonscape where there used to be a beautiful, fairy-tale little creek crossing my property. And I've lost the waterline and the access to my driveway. There are a few places where the mud climbed the bank and came mighty close to my storage area. But the only damage I can find is a truck canopy hit by a fallen tree. Even my junk piles are untouched! I feel totally blessed—the slide went right on by."

I was twitchy and nervous, needing to move. "Come on," I said to Christopher, "let's keep going. I really want to see our place." Kurt joined our party and the five of us crossed his driveway and stepped out onto the moonscape.

It was impossible to get one's bearings. All the trees were gone. All the shortcut trails and the mossy forest floor had been erased, smothered with sticky mud, laced with boulders and tangled timbers. The power of the slide was evident: trees had been pulverized into short lengths with rounded ends, ripped clean of bark. Boulders the size of cars lay scattered like marbles.

What trees were these that stood at the edge of the landslide path? I no longer knew them. They reeled drunkenly. Some supported fallen comrades. Others gesticulated at the universe with stumps of limbs, blindly seeking answers. Their trunks were clotted with mud, deeply gouged and bleeding sap. Exposed now to the full force of the elements, they looked vulnerable, traumatized and bereft. They were survivors like us; scarred warriors on a muddy battlefield.

I paused to put on my rubber beach shoes before climbing over the muddy bank. We stayed north of the slide path, found an old overgrown trail down to the lake, then emerged onto the beach and waded across Gar Creek. An enormous fan-shaped delta lay at the mouth of the new creek outflow.

But the house! Where was it? All I could see was an earthy mound, some bunched timbers, an edging of deck and a bit of roof held against two brave old fir trees that had somehow stood strong. I recognized those trees. I used to gaze up at them from my lounge chair on the deck. The swallow had perched on the top dead snag every evening. Where were those swallows now? Their young certainly had not yet fledged last Thursday morning.

I began to understand how the trajectory and timing of the second slide had saved Osa and me. At first, the waves of liquid mud had followed the old creek bed, curving to the south of the house. But after a matter of seconds the force and magnitude of the mudslide had broken through the bank and taken a new path to the lake, straight downhill from Kurt's driveway, north of us. Those first brief moments before the slide divided in two had given us precious seconds to get back into the boat. The place where we'd stood on the shore was unrecognizable: a treeless gravel delta.

We picked our way cautiously between broken branches and boulders, our feet held fast and sucked downward by the silty mud. Christopher and Roger began to poke at the fingers of cracked timber, plywood, roofing and shreds of pink insulation. Every few moments one of us would exclaim at a discovery: the stainless steel chimney, like a cylinder of crumpled kitchen foil, lay several metres from the main wreckage; our orchard ladder had become a twisted metal filigree; white ceramic briquettes out of the barbecue lay scattered in the gravel.

One week ago, at around this time in the early afternoon, I'd crouched on the deck, weaving a trellis for Christopher's sweet peas. I looked up at the line of deck edging, just visible, sandwiched between layers of mud. Those hours at work on the shady deck, I now recognized, had been my last moments of peaceful perfection. Ozzie had been beside me, watching every move I made. The gentle breeze had rustled the leaves, the late afternoon sun sparkled off the water, the ospreys wheeled and called across the lake, and the swallows toiled back and forth overhead.

LEAVING THE OTHERS to their forensics, Carol and I climbed onward, below the house, south towards Christopher's up-ended driftwood trees. An official had nailed an evacuation zone warning onto one of them. The lake level had dropped at least a metre but the beach was non-negotiable—a dense tangle of ripped-out trees lay in heaps and floated over the water. Our beach path was untouched and led up from the beach to the driveway, the post office cabin and the fenced garden. I opened the driftwood gate and looked inside. The fence was intact, but the walkways were almost impassable with mud. Instead of raised beds criss-crossed by bark-mulch paths, the garden now had a uniformly flat surface, the beds framed by concrete-grey "pavement" studded with bark bits. The pea pods were swollen, perfect for picking, and I stepped through the gate. I sank up to my ankles and almost toppled over. Christopher had warned me about this.

The flower garden greeted me with arrays of colourful blooms: pink and white phlox, blood-red dahlias, golden calendula and day lilies, foxgloves, poppies, delphiniums. But their cheery faces jarred with my mood and I turned away, unable to bear the sight of them. Across the driveway from the post office cabin stood our mauve and purple picnic table and the vase of peonies and foxgloves, now drooping and forlorn, that I'd put there exactly a week ago. How had the vase not even fallen over? Beyond the picnic table everything stopped at the wall of earth, rocks and chunks of wood that blocked the driveway, higher than the cabin roof.

I stood transfixed by the wall and its dark meaning. The special trees that Ruth Burt had planted during thirty years on that land all lay directly in the path of the landslide. Every last one had been destroyed. Christopher, inspired by Ruth's vision of "studied decadence" as he called it, had taken over her stewardship duties after we moved into her house in 1993. He cut back the birches to give her California redwood tree more light and air. He planted the Japanese maple that stood beside the front door. Under the maple, on a flat grey rock, sat our Buddha, small, silvery and cross-legged, with a gap between one arm and his lap where I used to place tiny bouquets of flowers, moss or twigs. Where was he now?

The flower bed outside the front door had been a wild area where purple crocus pushed up in spring, and big blue bellflowers bloomed in early summer. Elderberry, periwinkle, cotoneaster and sedum all had their special places. A curved driftwood border edged the bed, wide and comfortable to sit on in the shade of the apple tree, while Ozzie rolled in the soft grass at our feet. Christopher had worked patiently for more than fifteen years, transforming his landscaping dreams into substance. He'd moved tons of soil, placed boulders and driftwood, hired a backhoe operator to dig waterline trenches and created a sloping "glade" down to the creek.

In spring 2012, Christopher had planted a new pale pink variety of heather named Amanda alongside the hosta and iris clumps, close to the creek. Ruth bequeathed us a quince bush we carefully transplanted, which rewarded our care every spring with ever more abundant burgundy blossoms. Ruth had left her mark with perennial poppies, columbine, day lilies, forsythia, wild roses and buddleia.

How wasted their efforts seemed, crushed and buried in an instant. Every one of those named and nurtured plants was dead, along with the dreams Ruth and Christopher had cherished for the property. Standing there beside the slide, I acknowledged that Ruth's legacy to the future had been erased and that her magical garden, as well as her house—our home—really had disappeared forever.

Carol put her hand gently on my shoulder and roused me from my reverie. "Come on, let's set the table for lunch." I found a rag in the cabin, dipped it in the lake and we cleaned the twigs and grit off the table. After wiping it down, we unpacked our picnic supplies. I put out the plastic tub of pasta salad, celery and carrot sticks, and a water bottle. Carol contributed a bag of snow peas fresh from her garden, a hummus dip, corn chips and cookies.

We called Christopher, Roger and Kurt, and sat down to eat. I took a photo of my four shell-shocked companions that afterwards struck me as surreal—eating a picnic in front of what looked like a movie set from a dystopian film of otherworldly devastation. They looked like ghosts. I don't know how we could even eat, talk or walk.

After lunch I had only one goal in mind: to strip off my muddy clothes and get into the water. For twenty years I had swum naked in this lake, loving the way the water caressed my skin. Today I was here and I was going swimming. Carol came in with me but I soon lost sight of her among the drifting logs. Once in the water I slipped between the smooth tree trunks, dived under the debris and made my way back to the mouth of Gar Creek. The creek was running clean again, and the dreadful smell no longer hung in the air. I don't know why I felt less vulnerable in the water than out of it; I certainly couldn't have swum clear in time if another slide had come down. Yet I lingered there for nearly half an hour exploring the creek mouth and shoreline.

I plunged underwater and examined the sandy delta. Pieces of water pipe, black, anaconda-like, swayed in the current. I watched, fascinated. Kurt's and our water intakes had been flushed down the creek. There had to be hundreds more metres of black plastic pipe nearby. Coming up to the surface for air I heard Carol calling my name with an urgency in her voice. My heart did a double flip. An emergency? Another slide? I began a fast crawl away from the delta, back to our beach. Carol looked anxious. "I couldn't see you and wondered if something had happened."

"No, it's okay. I always spend ages in the water once I'm in." Reluctantly I left the lake's embrace and lay down in the sun to dry. This used to be my life every hot summer's day, working up a sweat in the garden then plunging into the water to cool off, sunbathing perhaps longer than I should, and beachcombing naked along the shore. Even at the height of summer I was often the only person down here, kept company by otters, loons and occasional coyotes. How was I going to adjust to a life without freedom to roam wild and naked?

Dressed again, I found Christopher on his hands and knees, next to his storage shed, just below the road. The slide had swept down behind the shed, pushed it several metres and demolished the structure, but many of the contents were visible. He was attempting to prise twisted metal bicycle parts out from under the collapsed walls. He looked hot and preoccupied, and when I greeted him his voice was monotone, despairing. Things weren't going well, but he wanted a bit more time to work on it.

Carol and I walked down to the beach turnaround. This section of the road was almost its old self, but the surface was deeply fissured—gushing water had gouged mini gulleys as it sought a new route to the lake, in the twenty-four hours between the two landslides. Otherwise, the scenery was unchanged. Bizarre to look one way and see complete familiarity; in the other direction I was lost without landmarks, in an alien country.

The sun was dipping low towards the ridge. I'd seen enough and urgently wanted to go home. Carol stuck close, taking care of me, distracting me, encouraging me. She and Roger needed to get home and I told her I'd be fine. I'd wait for Christopher in the post office cabin. Inside, I found Renata's clothes neatly folded on shelves and her food in jars and containers. The fridge stank because the power line had been ripped out, and I emptied the rotting perishables into a grocery bag. No need to attract a bear down here.

The Tiger by John Vaillant lay on the table. We'd lent it to Renata in June. By lending it out we'd saved it from the landslide: the only volume left. It was a wonderful book about the wild Siberian tigers of Russia's far east, and the hardy folk who inhabited that remote corner of the country. Vaillant's prose was breathtaking in its eloquence. I sat down on the couch, opened the book to Ren's marked page, and read:

> The first impact of a tiger attack does not come from the tiger itself, but from the roar, which, in addition to being loud like a jet, has an eerie capacity to fill the space around it, leaving one unsure where to look. From close range, the experience is overwhelming, and has the effect of separating you from yourself, of scrambling the very neurology that is supposed to save you at times like this. Those who have done serious tiger time—scientists and hunters—describe the tiger's roar not as a sound so much as a full-body experience. Sober, disciplined biologists have sworn they felt the earth shake. One Russian hunter, taken by surprise, recalled thinking that a dam had burst somewhere. In short, the tiger's roar exists in the same sonic realm as a natural catastrophe; it is one of those sounds that give meaning and substance to "the fear of God."

I stopped reading. Vaillant's words gave me the tiniest inkling of what Val, Diana, Rachel and Petra might have experienced when they'd heard that roar, a noise so all-encompassing it incapacitated the hearer. I could only begin to imagine their panic and terror.

Christopher put his head around the door. He was filthy, tired and hungry. We hiked back to Roger and Carol's, and were delighted and grateful to be invited for dinner. Carol took me to their bedroom, where she'd laid out heaps of clothes for me to rummage through. So much that had been taken away from us was now being restored in abundance. I greatly appreciated the outpouring of kindness and generosity from all sides; it warmed my heart and comforted me.

PHOTO: FRANCIS SILVAGGIO

Before leaving for Kaslo that morning I cut some foxgloves and peonies and placed them in a vase on the mauve picnic table. Next morning, only minutes before the second landslide, Francis Silvaggio took this photo of them.

Chapter 4: Dreams and Portents

Two DAYS LATER, with Christopher gone on yet another trip to the Landing, I invited my niece Margie Smith, Ren's middle daughter, and her lifelong friend Lila Taylor round for tea. It was good to see the girls walking up the path together: Margie, dark-haired and tall, Lila, petite and blonde. To me these two beautiful young women were like a breath of exotic air, poised and graceful in summery cotton dresses that floated and hugged their slim figures.

Their youthful spirit and sweetness brought much needed lighter energy into our sad house and lifted my mood; I'd been despondent ever since our trip to the Landing on Thursday. They embraced me warmly, settled into chairs and asked after us with interest and concern. I told them a bit about our trip on Thursday, how awful and sad it had been to see the destruction. "It's so ugly and alien up there. I could hardly recognize it as being the Landing."

I offered my condolences on the loss of their best friend, Diana. Margie and Lila smiled sad smiles, but they seemed serene, peaceful and somehow accepting. Margie said, "We're hoping they'll start digging again. It would be wonderful if they could find Rachel too, in time for the memorial next Saturday."

I brought a pot of Earl Grey tea from the kitchen, and some delicate bone china cups and saucers, mismatched but still pretty. The girls exclaimed over the china and teased me playfully for my insistence on traditional English teatime habits. We tucked into cake and cookies—store-bought, I was ashamed to admit, but I was not up to home baking yet.

Margie and Lila, along with other young friends, were busy organizing the memorial service. Lynn Migdal—Diana and Rachel's mother—had been in Kaslo for a week since flying in from her home in Florida. Margie and Lila, like daughters to her, were assisting in every way they could. They'd stayed with her at the Kaslo Motel for her first few nights, and the three of them were now in a nearby rental cabin provided by the Red Cross.

"I'm so grateful you found time to pop by when you've got so much else going on," I said. But I had other reasons for wanting to talk to them because I'd heard some mystifying reports from Renata about Margie and Lila, concerning strange things the girls had experienced. I was puzzled and intrigued, but felt suddenly shy now that they were sitting here beside me. I raised the subject, tentatively. "I wanted to ask if you'd be willing to tell me a bit more about those odd things that happened to you...?" They both nodded and Lila said they'd like very much to tell me their stories.

Margie had moved to Vancouver to work as a nanny. She and Diana, who lived in Los Angeles, kept in close contact, talked often on the phone and discussed everything. Cradling her teacup, Margie looked away into the distance and closed her eyes for a moment. She took a deep breath and plunged in. "One night at the end of May I had a dream in which I saw the landslide." She paused and looked at me. "It was a crazy dream. I was watching from twenty feet above the Webbers' garage, the one building that wasn't covered. I saw the whole thing come down, just the way it is now. I watched it cover Diana's house, knowing they were all inside. I knew the whole family had died.

"The detail was remarkable. I distinctly remember watching the landslide reach Harvey's pottery house. You know, I loved that house because I'd lived there as a child. It was my first real home. The slide came right up to it, didn't touch it, but continued onward in a 'nose' of material that hit the Webbers' house instead. The roof and walls were ripped away and I saw the roof floating in a sea of mud."

Margie sighed and leaned back.

I asked what happened next.

"I telephoned Diana and told her everything. I said, 'I dreamed that your house was buried in mud and you were all inside.' We discussed the dream but didn't make too much of it. It wasn't something we were going to worry about. She was in Los Angeles, Rachel was in Kaslo and Lynn was in Florida, so it seemed unlikely that the whole family could be about to die in the Johnson's Landing house."

Margie and Diana had wondered if thoughts of the snow avalanche in February might perhaps have prompted the dream. There was no way of telling.

Lila spoke up. "Six weeks later, just two days before the landslide, Diana told me about Margie's dream. We were out in Val's rowboat, having one of those silly conversations about how we thought we might die. Maybe in a forest fire? Maybe in a flood? Diana said, 'Margie had a dream that my house was buried under mud.' We laughed about it, but it was one of several things that afterwards felt very significant. Another was when we found Diana's camera in the slide; the last photo she'd taken was a shot from out on the water, zoomed right in on the spot where the slide began."

I gazed at the two girls and rubbed the goosebumps on my arms. What possible explanation could there be for something as incredible as this? Margie's dream had been uncannily detailed and accurate. The slide had indeed passed alongside Harvey Armstrong's pottery studio and his rental house next door, knocking them off-kilter and doing a lot of damage, but leaving them entirely visible.

I grappled for some kind of response. "If Time is a dimension, maybe it's a bit like a helix. Maybe Time spirals round us, so that you, Margie, asleep in May, somehow caught a glimpse of the curl of Time six weeks ahead, and the future disaster it held." I had no other explanation to offer.

Lila broke the silence as I refilled their cups. "That's not the only weird thing that happened. On Friday, the day of the second landslide, I left the Landing and went to our house in Nelson to get away from everything. That evening I was sitting on the back porch. I was in a bad way. I felt terrible. Self-destructive. I didn't want to eat or shower. I just wanted to hide in a hole and not see anyone.

"All of a sudden I had what I can only describe as a 'connection' with Diana. Nothing like it had ever happened to me before. I heard Diana's voice inside my head. She said: 'Don't be upset. When you are emotional I can't come through to you. I need to warn you, because you are the one who will first get this news: my body is going to be in rough shape when they find it. It's not a bad thing that's happened. We are all fine now, but Rachel had a hard time because of how she died.'

"'People need you to be strong. You and Margie are the face, out there in the community dealing with everyone. Make an effort to connect with others. Otherwise it will be harder for them. I am going to show up in different forms and signs, and you'll have to guess!'"

Lila's bright blue eyes shone as she turned to me and smiled. "I was so comforted, hearing her voice. I'm definitely not into psychic stuff, but this felt real. I'd lost Diana's physical presence, yet in some ways she felt even more present—I could talk to her at any point. Knowing she wasn't gone gave me the strength and courage I needed. I'd never thought about these kinds of things before."

Lila's blonde hair fell forward like a curtain as she looked down and moved crumbs around on her plate. I offered her more cake but she shook her head, flicked back her hair and went on. "In the car with Renata the next morning, on the way to Castlegar airport to meet Margie, I told Ren about my connection with Diana. I was in the process of repeating the exact words Diana had used—about showing up in different forms—when, at that precise moment, an enormous bald eagle swooped low, wings outstretched, and practically skimmed the top of the car. And there have been other moments since then when I've known, *That was Diana!*"

"Wow!" Renata had already told me about the eagle, like a jumbo jet, heading straight for them, low over her car, and what a powerful moment it had been.

Further proof that Diana's words had been prophetic came on Monday, July 16, while Lila, her mother, Susan, and Margie were with Lynn at the Kaslo Motel. Sergeant Tim Little of the RCMP came to the door and asked if he might speak to Lila outside. He told her they'd found Diana's body, but it was dismembered. As Diana had forewarned, her physical body was "in rough shape," and Lila was the one who received the news.

Now both girls talked at once. Signs in abundance had revealed themselves at the Webber house site. Heart-shaped rocks appeared everywhere. Lila laughed, and said, "I see hearts all the time now, in all forms of nature. There are so many! We put the heart rocks on a large boulder. Bob Stair found Diana's body right beside that boulder—it's her tombstone."

Margie explained about the "mud-pages," as she called them: fragments torn out of books, found lying in the gravelly soil nearby. Some contained eerily significant phrases. One tiny scrap of a page read: "and they sat down for breakfast. After breakfast…" There the fragment ended. Another page they picked up started with the words, "and they buried him in the mud."

Lila said, "I feel she's guiding us, giving us little messages along the way. I sense her presence; it's a strong connection."

We moved to the living room, made ourselves comfortable on the couches and Lila filled me in on Diana's last days. She'd driven up from Los Angeles, arriving about a week before the landslide. Overjoyed to see one another, the two had made lots of plans for the summer. Diana also spent a couple of days in Kaslo with Rachel, who had a rental house there and a summer job at the Kaslo Motel.

On the day before the landslide, Diana had driven Rachel back to the Landing so they could spend time together with their dad.

Lila had seen Diana for the last time that Wednesday evening, while she and Carol were canoeing. Diana, in Val's green rowboat, pulled alongside and the three women talked for a few minutes. Lila then said Diana had phoned her on Thursday morning, only minutes before the landslide, and *that* had been very odd too. But before she could tell me why, Margie looked at her watch and quietly interrupted. "I'm so sorry, but we really need to get going." They were already late for an appointment and still had lots to do to prepare for next Saturday's memorial in Argenta. Margie gave me an advance copy of the card they'd designed.

I waved them off at the front door. "Thank you so much for coming over. We'll see you next Saturday."

I sat down at the table, the memorial card in my hand, with its colour photos of Petra, Val, Diana and Rachel on the front. A poem by Diana was printed on the back.

My head was spinning. Portents in dreams. Psychic connections. I knew for a fact that such things did happen. My brother, Andrew, had had an inexplicable connection with our dad just after he'd died. We'd been searching fruitlessly through Daddy's papers for some important documents. In the night, Andrew was roused by a swirling, emotion-laden energy field of both anger and sadness, and his hands were guided to the place where the documents lay, well hidden in the middle of an ancient advertising brochure about double-glazing windows.

We haven't the slightest idea how these deeper, intangible aspects of the universe work. Rational science will probably never explain life's manifold mysteries.

I read Diana's poem:

If you follow the highway
To where the highway ends
And then rough it for several miles on the dirt road
Until it ends
You might stumble upon a small,
Barely visible sign bearing the words
'JOHNSON'S LANDING. Unincorporated'

A home at the end of the road...

If you love a place
In the way that you love a person,
I have surely known no love
Like I have known for Johnson's Landing.

KASLO AND THE other communities at the north end of Kootenay Lake were in limbo. They wanted the body of seventeen-year-old Rachel Webber found. But five days after Chief Coroner Lisa Lapointe had put the recovery mission on hold, it was still suspended. Behind the scenes, Bob Stair, the local coroner and incident commander, was in close communication with Lapointe. They were long-time colleagues. Bob, a tall, energetic figure and keen mountain climber, urged Lapointe to allow him one or two more days to excavate. He was confident that he could find Rachel's body. He had a clear idea where it must be.

Bob had led the team that recovered Val and Diana Webber's bodies. He instructed the excavators to start at the side of the slide, at a point reasonably close to Val's house. They dug from the edge and the material out-flowed behind them.

Although Bob had worked in many types of terrain, the Johnson's Landing landslide was a first for him for several reasons. The material had been laid down only two days previously. It was saturated with water and contained enormous trees, and boulders too large for the excavators to move easily.

The mud was gooey clay: it oozed and crept forward as they dug. They could not dig a vertical face or cliff, but had to bevel the top surface of the pile, to prevent it caving in on the exposed area underneath. The deeper they dug, the greater were the logistical complexities and dangers.

The site of Petra Frehse's cabin presented enormous difficulties. The cabin lay under eight metres of unstable landslide material, in a location perilously close to Gar Creek. For four days, four excavators (including the biggest on site, a 330 Class), worked on the Frehse site, with a team of watchers for each machine. Enormous effort went into this complex excavation. And once they eventually reached ground level, it took dozens of bucketfuls from above to advance one bucketful forward.

They located Petra's house site, but the cabin was nowhere to be seen—they found only splinters of the huge log walls. "It looked as though the house had been exploded," Bob said later. They unearthed many artifacts but did not find Petra's body. Bob estimates it would have taken weeks to excavate completely, and they did not have the luxury of weeks to complete the task.

But he could find Rachel. He knew it.

Bob Stair had his team ready on call and had drawn up a small budget to cover two days' work. The site was becoming somewhat safer now that the rains had let up. All he needed now was permission from the chief coroner.

Chapter 5: Recovery and Memorial

THE MEETING IN the Kaslo Legion Hall on Monday, July 23, was held to update the public about the work being done, road repairs, site safety and next steps. People poured in and clustered around poster-sized aerial shots of the landslide pinned to the wall. Paul rolled his wheelchair alongside us, and beckoned to Bob Stair, his old mountain-climbing buddy, who was pacing up and down at the back. Paul asked Bob how things were going. Bob gave a thumbs-up sign and lowered his voice. "I got it. I got permission this afternoon." We congratulated him. "I had a hard time juggling the budget, but everyone wanted to make this happen. People volunteered their time and now the cost looks reasonable." Bob's perseverance, and his contacts in the Coroners Service, had paid off.

He was the first to address the crowd and told us he was making final preparations; his team would be back at work first thing in the morning. The audience cheered. Bob then apologized for leaving. Applause, calls of encouragement and good wishes followed him out.

The logistical operation that had been going on in Johnson's Landing over the past ten days was enormous. The road had been rebuilt using a huge culvert, with a two-and-a-half-metre diameter, brought in from Vancouver. Electricity and phone services had been restored to all but one inhabited household. Geomorphologists were examining the mountainside to try to understand how the landslide had happened and predict future danger.

The most urgent priority for residents on the south side of the Landing was a reliable water supply. The water intake lines and distribution box had been destroyed and it would cost a great deal of money to establish a new water system for the thirteen out of eighteen households that remained habitable.

People in Kaslo donated jugs and bottles of water from the first day, thanks, in part, to the community Facebook page, which allowed individuals travelling north to post meet-up times for water donation. Andy Shadrack had delivered a flat of bottled water to the community hall. Lake water was pumped into tanks and trucked to people's houses. But these fixes were only temporary. Kootenay Joe Farm needed water for crop irrigation and for the animals. Extensive vegetable gardens sustained homesteads year-round. The rain had ceased, the summer sun was beating down and the hillside was drying out fast. Soon it would be forest fire season.

THE NEXT DAY, Bob led a team that included Kaslo Search and Rescue manager Bruce Walker, RCMP corporal Chris Backus, local excavator-operator Duncan Lake and Larry Badry of the BC Ambulance Service. They excavated at the Webbers' house for two full days. One month exactly after Rachel's seventeenth birthday, on Wednesday, July 25, at around six p.m., they found her body a short distance away from where her father and sister were found.

Afterwards, Corporal Chris Backus expressed deep admiration for Bob's diligence each time human remains were uncovered. "Bob would stop the heavy machinery and get in with hand tools. It was like a very delicate archaeological dig. The bodies were long deceased but Bob treated them with the utmost dignity. He recovered each one as if they were his own kin."

In a press release, Lisa Lapointe paid tribute to all who had assisted the recovery mission. "Special thanks must go to all the volunteers from Kaslo Search and Rescue and their manager Bruce Walker, to the local ambulance, fire and RCMP members, our colleagues at Emergency Management BC, and to forensic analyst Bob Stair, who pinpointed with such accuracy the best locations to search... Additionally, we would like to thank the people of Kaslo and surrounding areas for the support and many kindnesses they demonstrated throughout the search effort."

Lapointe reluctantly confirmed that no further efforts would be undertaken to try to locate Petra Frehse's body. A sizeable excavation had been completed at the site of her former residence, but "due to the catastrophic impact of the slide at that site, the experts have concluded that there is no reasonable likelihood of locating her."

Later, Bob Stair told me that, in his opinion, the four victims died instantly. He explained that a landslide isn't like an earthquake, where people sometimes survive in pockets of safety under the wreckage of houses. A debris-flow landslide deposits material and rolls over the top of it. In a moment, the victims would have been knocked flat to the ground and buried. Very few seconds elapsed between the thunder of the slide's descent (likened by witnesses to the roar of a 747 jet) and its impact on the Webber house. The family probably had no more than twenty seconds to react, and Petra even less. Val and Diana's bodies were found outside on what had been the grass, in the lee of the house, where they had likely sought shelter. Rachel lay nearer to the front of the house.

THE MEMORIAL FOR Petra Frehse and Val, Diana and Rachel Webber took place in the Argenta Community Hall the afternoon of Saturday, July 28.

An osprey soaring over Argenta would see an unpaved gravel road that climbs steeply, then hairpins back on itself, cutting a line through the trees across the lower flank of Mount Willett. Homesteads mostly lie tucked away in the woods, out of sight of the road. Straw bale and stucco, cedar and rough plywood—every kind of habitation appears there, from shacks and pre-fabs to yurts and vaulted timber-frame log palaces. Each property has its patch of cleared ground for vegetables and flowers. Some have ponds and meadows. Workshops, pottery kilns and chicken coops hide among the trees.

It's hard to believe that over a hundred people live in Argenta: three times the population of the Landing. Farmers like Vince McIntyre, who ploughs with horses and grows our winter root vegetables. Quiet forest folk like the elderly Quakers, who light a fire in the hearth of the Friends Meeting House every Sunday morning and welcome all comers to silent worship.

This sunny Saturday afternoon, the air was filled with birdsong and the scent of drying hay. Sylvan trundled down the road on his tractor, seated in a perfect lotus pose, his long grey hair parted in two neat braids that framed his boyish face. His machine rattled past the Argenta post office, a rough-hewn shed next to the hall—a humble building maybe, but the beating heart of the community. A pair of young men in dreadlocks sat on a bench outside, under the notice board, whittling wood. The board displayed rain-smudged, handwritten notes that advertised fresh eggs, hay bales, work wanted, ride shares to Nelson and calls to oppose the development of the Jumbo Glacier ski resort.

The door of the post office opened and three small beige and white goats trotted out, their dainty hooves clicking like stilettos on the wooden boardwalk. A voice bellowed after them: "And stay out!" David Herbison, the postmaster, had opened up the office as a favour to someone who wanted their mail, even though it was Saturday. Usual business days were Monday, Wednesday and Friday. David gathered the goat-nibbled flyers off the floor, stood up and caught the strains of a song that drifted out of the hall's open doorways. His fine tenor voice took up the refrain and crooned in harmony with Frank Sinatra.

Two young women in Indian cotton dresses, babies slung on their backs, laughed and clapped at David's rendition, then stepped around the goats and peeped inside the hall. Argenta's hall is much larger than the one in Johnson's Landing. Built, enlarged and refurbished by the community over many years, the building had lately been re-roofed in red steel, with acoustic baffles installed on the ceiling to reduce the echo in the cavernous main room. Music of all kinds, and the recording of music, is important in Argenta. The hall easily accommodates a medium-sized orchestra, a production of Gilbert and Sullivan, a square dance for eighty, basketball, soccer, yoga, craft fairs, community events—and sombre gatherings such as the memorial.

People began to collect in the simple kitchen and dining area. Covered dishes of food accumulated on the counter. Two women, purposeful and efficient, prepared urns of coffee and boiled water for tea. A bearded man with elaborate tattoos across his naked back checked the small bathroom behind the kitchen, put out extra toilet paper and taped a sign to the wall, warning users to be gentle with the dodgy plumbing.

Downstairs, all was quiet. A wood-burning furnace stood cold and idle. It heated the building in winter, when people gathered in the cozy basement library for preschool, evening classes or just to socialize or read. Its well-stocked shelves, thanks to Ann MacNab and many other volunteers, held an imaginative selection of volumes and films on wide-ranging subjects. Unexpected in a tiny place like this, you might think—until you understood the ethos of Argenta. People home-schooled their children and avoided conventional medicine. Most lived off the land and grew their own food. They treasured their library.

It was cool inside the main hall, with all doors standing open to admit the gentle breeze. Lynn Migdal had arrived early with Margie, Lila and several other young friends. Memorial tables at the back of the room displayed photos, teddy bears, books and flowers in the glow of lighted candles.

Lynn had turned up the volume, and the room throbbed to the deep, sexy tones of Frank Sinatra. She'd found the music cassette in the garage, the one building untouched by the slide. The cassette held many family favourites, including songs by the Beatles, Joni Mitchell and Carole King.

Christopher and I also arrived early. I gave Lynn a big hug and said how sorry I was for everything that had happened. Lynn greeted me with a smile. She was wearing a simple black dress adorned with a heavy silver brooch and a colourful shawl. Her face was deeply lined, yet she appeared to be bearing up well, and almost exuberant, as people deep in the manic madness of grief so often are—dancing to the music, laughing with her daughters' friends as they dressed the walls with photographs and laid garlands of calendula flowers around the framed pictures on the tables. I knew from my work with bereavement clients for the hospice that her euphoria would pass.

The crowd swelled. The people came! On foot, by bicycle, even on horseback. And not just from Argenta and the Landing. A neatly parked line of shimmering metal stretched away on both sides of the road for nearly a kilometre. People trudged the hot dusty road from ever more remote parking spots, in muddy hiking boots, bare feet, homemade sandals, Nike trainers and leather court shoes. Kate O'Keefe and Harvey Armstrong from the Landing. John and Jillian Madill, now staying at Ann MacNab's house in Howser. Greg Utzig and Donna MacDonald from Nelson. Bill Wells and ML Thomson from Kaslo. Gail and Lynne, Roger and Carol, Kurt and so many others. Media people in a white van lurked outside in the sun, fishing for interviews, but were politely rebuffed.

The congregation climbed the wooden steps, greeted friends, shooed away various excited dogs that ran in and out. They slipped inside, gratefully grabbed glasses of water from the kitchen, mopped their brows and circulated around the room, fanning themselves with the memorial card and looking at photos. Eventually they chose their seats and sat down. Chairs scraped on the floor. Everyone settled and a hush descended.

Latecomers stood in the doorways and along the porch. A sea of expectant faces gazed up at the microphones and at the huge bouquets of fresh-picked flowers in vases on the makeshift stage. A few people held hands. Others clutched tissues. Some were already crying.

The girls had planned a simple, moving "Celebration of Life." Many people gave readings and shared remembrances. A slide show accompanied by Lynn's music cassette concluded the formal proceedings. The audience sighed over family snapshots of smiling faces; of children playing in the meadow and on the beach; the girls growing up into young adults; of Petra smiling sweetly against a backdrop of snow-capped mountains and sparkling lake. We mourned the four souls lost, and we mourned for Johnson's Landing and its former loveliness.

The memorial ceremony was followed by a huge potluck meal. Everyone was ravenous; crying is exhausting work. We tucked into roast turkey, baked salmon, a lamb moussaka, chicken enchiladas, tofu, baked vegetables, devilled eggs and every imaginable salad. Then dessert. The kitchen clattered with activity, as empty platters were removed and new dishes emerged; there was more than enough to feed the enormous gathering.

When it was time to leave, Christopher negotiated out of the scrum of parked vehicles and we headed down the road. At the junction with Argenta Hill he automatically turned left, south towards Johnson's Landing, then realized his mistake.

Chapter 6: Excavation

Our home awaited us
Tenderly took us in
Enfolded us in its singular perfume
Offered its feline friend for our solace
Cached our food
Delivered our water
Slept us
Guarded our dreams
Woke us
Soothed us
Befriended our friends
Demanded from us
Oh yes! Demanded from us
Accosted us with its random smells
Held its breath aghast when we argued
Lit our skulls with its suffusion of afternoon sun
Murmured encouragement as we made love
Enchanted us with its colony of little brown bats
Creeped us out with its big black ants
Arched its back to protect us from the pummelling rain
Held tough under months of heavy snow
Stretched its bones as we walked its floors at dawn
Gave surface to a dozen rainbows sent
From a crystal twisting in the morning sun.

This Kootenay cabin
Planned with anticipation
Built by many hands
In turns both hastily thrown together
And laboriously crafted into existence—
Was reduced.
With the force of immeasurable tons
And the languorous lapse of four seconds
Our home was reduced
From all it had been and so much more
To a tomb of dismembered dreams
And unfathomable nightmares.

In its humiliation and ruin
And to the detriment of the treasure it held
Our house waited.
Its people had to decide.
They had to listen to advice.
They had to mourn their dead.
They had to bide their time while behemoth machinery
Finished other more pressing tasks.

Patiently it waited
Holding for us a promise
Dark and rebundled.

—Christopher Klassen

CHRISTOPHER WAS ON a crusade. He'd decided early on, while driving back from Eugene, that he would—he must—excavate our house. When I questioned him and argued, he frowned. "Babe, I *have* to do this. If I don't, I'll spend the rest of my life wondering what we might have saved."

I agreed that, indeed, there was longed-for treasure under the mud, but my thinking was purely selfish; the only things

I figured I wanted were Macaroon the MacBook (for the files on the hard drive) and the beige filing cabinet from the bedroom that held my mother's and my jewellery. Yet Christopher, too, had lost countless precious things, not least of which were his lifetime collections of photography, and his fine woodworking tools. But the house lay smack in the middle of the slide path—one of the most hazardous spots in the entire evacuation zone—and Christopher wanted to dig a hole there.

"How long do you think it will take?" I asked hesitantly.

"Hard to say. Duncan's going to phone me when he's ready. He'll bring his machine down the hill as soon as he finishes the berm above Petra's and the trench for the new waterline on the south side. He says he'll charge us the minimum, just to cover his costs. He might dig for three, perhaps four days. But it all depends on what we find." His eyes were bright. He was animated and more positive than he'd been in weeks. A man fired up by a mission.

I wished I could share his excitement but the landslides had swept away my trust in our mountainside, my sense of safety and equilibrium. No longer grounded, I was aimless, shaky and unbalanced in my thinking. We'd been busy in the immediate aftermath of the disaster and I'd managed to function. But now I brooded, engulfed by hopelessness.

Peter Jordan, a geotechnical expert with the Ministry of Forests, dubbed the first landslide a "one-in-a-million" event, exceptionally big by comparison with others in the province. British Columbia sees many landslides on its steep mountainsides, but most occur in isolated, uninhabited valleys with no risk to people or property. Three weeks on, technical experts speculated that a substantial volume of unstable debris was still "hanging" at the source area above the Landing community. A portion of it had slipped twenty metres and stopped—it was a scary-looking slumped area visible to the naked eye, with a sandy border around it. Another landslide as big as the one we'd just suffered might come down at any point, so they said. We shuddered every time it rained.

The evacuation order continued in force. How foolish was it to defy the authorities, ignore the roadblock and work for days, maybe weeks, in the alluvial fan beside the creek? I understood, however, the helplessness Christopher was feeling, told he couldn't do anything, shouldn't do anything, couldn't go back.

CHRISTOPHER LATER SCRIBBLED down a few thoughts about the events of August. Eloquent and simple, his words helped me understand what the excavation meant to him, and what it was like to be there. I include his voice, in italics, to help me tell this part of our story.

Obliterated as it was, we could have walked away. Had our home burned we'd have had no option. Through burial, however, it was an uneven subtraction. There was a remainder. It tantalized with possibility and drove my imagination into a confusion of hope and despair.

Christopher's first task was to locate the house, when all reference points and landmarks were gone. He needed an expert in satellite positioning and mapping, and Greg Utzig, our friend and Landing neighbour, stepped forward to assist. He used an orthophoto of the house taken before the slide (an aerial picture, geo-rectified to remove distortion and produce an accurate map) to obtain latitude and longitude readings for each corner. Greg and his GPS met Christopher on the earthy expanse beside the creek.

Measuring tape and recollection had no purchase. Our landscape had been erased and renewed. Only by satellite and electronic wizardry could we again find our place in the world. We stuck bits of branch in the ground and flagged them with bright tape. Four points on a muddy field. Could this really be its orientation? Was that really our western view? Did we see so far south on Davis Ridge? Were those cottonwood trees really that far east?

Only one way to answer those questions.

On Thursday, August 2, Duncan Lake walked his large yellow Hyundai excavator down the creek gulley, heedless of danger. The digging began. Christopher decided to make the first plunge into the basement laundry room, an area holding little that the excavator might damage. Down they went, wood cracking and splintering, *the thudding of the hardened steel bucket on hollow structure, the screaming of steel crawler track on idler and driven cog, and the incessant growl of diesel.* Plywood layers of roof, then the kitchen floor, were rent asunder. The bucket bit into the hole, rose, spun off to the side, spewed its contents and spun back for more.

At fourteen feet the bucket claw came up with an olive green sheet of metal. Oh! I know what that is! It's the top to a filing cabinet, impaled like tissue paper. That means we missed the mark by ten feet to the south, and we're exactly on line to the east. Way to go, Greg!

Christopher watched, eagle-eyed, as the hole widened. The bucket made contact with something and he heard a rubbery *pop!* A burst tire. Then he saw the chassis, another wheel, crushed gold-brown bodywork—Jerald! Our ancient Toyota Tercel lay buried vertically, hood downward, over the basement. The slide must have pushed it from its parking spot outside the carport, around in an arc to the east wall of the house. When the walls collapsed and the floor separated from the foundation, Jerald plunged into the void. The digger's giant maw grabbed hold of the twisted metal body, lifted it skyward and shook it. A cascade of tools rained down into the hole.

Jerald was as totalled as a car could be. Crumpled into a ball, almost unrecognizable as a vehicle. But our faithful old friend had protected several bags of Christopher's most often used tools.

Finally the digger stopped. It trundled up the hill and away to serve other unfortunates. Its screeching and clattering dwindled to the point of silence and I was left alone under a blue sky, puffs of white cloud, the expanse and satisfaction of Kootenay Lake laid out before me to both north and south. The meditative quiet was broken only by the thud *and* clink *of my pick and shovel as I probed yet another corner of hell.*

Over the next five days Christopher and company explored the hole with hand tools. Duncan returned and expanded the opening to include the kitchen area. They also attacked the northwest corner—the bedroom. Between excavation days, Duncan's machine often stood parked in the meadow, the bucket lowered, like a long-necked yellow dinosaur cropping the grass.

By reason of both time and resource, we had to limit the excavation to those areas of greatest potential return. But how to find those specific areas? The house was toppled and smeared. How to figure out which flow of mud and debris pushed which way, and how far did it push? What about those logs of every imaginable diameter and length that subverted the flow patterns? As with a Rubik's Cube, how do you start without covering the next excavation with the tailings of the last?"

Much dirt was moved more than once over the next three weeks. Our neighbour Clint Carlson brought his backhoe to the site on August 9 and continued to dig in the northwest corner bedroom area, confident that they'd soon unearth the beige filing cabinet. They found the bedroom floor, the desk stool and the plank desk, one end of which had rested on the filing cabinet. They found a cardboard box of onions that had been on the floor alongside the filing cabinet. We even ate some of them. But the filing cabinet itself wasn't there.

Christopher was a man obsessed—horrified yet fascinated, repelled but drawn back. *The digger smashed its way through the compressed layers of our home, producing greater ruin and startling revelation in equal measure. Nineteen out of twenty bits of a former life now lay in shards, splinters, mould and mud. But the twentieth! Ho, man! An entire object to be treasured and held dear as a fellow survivor and talisman from a former life.*

Solitary items survived to be lifted whole and celebrated. A few tools. A single purple Fiestaware plate. One green cereal bowl with an intact Minnesota coffee mug nestling inside it as though seeking its protection. Some utensils out of the kitchen drawer, only slightly bent.

Christopher found and brought home to Kaslo my most recent journal. Delighted, I tore the damp pages out and laid them on the living room carpet to dry. The entries covered the first half of 2012, including my last trip to England, and recorded my joy at getting home in early July. The last words, dated Tuesday, July 10, were: "No work this week so I can continue to self-indulge. Ren will come sometime today or tomorrow."

Many of Christopher's slides and photographs emerged from boxes in the basement, in reasonably good shape. He found his egg-shaped eMac computer, its thick glass screen exploded in pieces. Kurt used grinding tools to cut through the metal innards and extract the hard drive. Later, in the Nelson Apple store, the data was found to be uncorrupted and Christopher retrieved more than five thousand digital photos.

Piles of shattered plastic cases arrived in Kaslo containing CDs that were powdery with dry mud, their paper inserts glued fast to the discs. I painstakingly washed each one with soap and warm water, taking care not to scratch the surface any further, then dried and tested them. Almost my entire collection of J.S. Bach returned to me, but the Goldberg Variations CD sounded quite mad. Both Fauré's and Mozart's Requiem Masses were unscathed—fitting musical tributes to commemorate the end of an era.

Again I found myself on hands and knees with my face just inches from the stinking muck of the basement floor, peering into a triangle of darkness that had been winking at me for days. One of so many black voids—some led nowhere; others extended many feet distant. They were as if to peer into a past and unattainable world.

Back as far as I could barely reach, a protruding corner with a lighter cast to it was suspended from above, clear of the slop covering the floor. I buried my arm to the shoulder and got hold of it. I wiggled it a bit but it wouldn't give. I persisted and the wiggling became a kind of sliding back and forth. I pulled harder, lathered shoulder to toe in stinking brown pudding slime. As my efforts increased I gained a better idea of what I actually had a hold of. My extracting frenzy redoubled.

Finally, pop! *It let go. I pulled it out and was stunned. All the books on that shelf had been lost to muck and mildew but this greatest favourite had returned to me. Yes, a bit misshapen but I had it in my hands:* The House at Pooh Corner!

Ho. Hum. Tiddly. Pom.

RENATA WENT TO the Landing to help her brother. Later she said, "I wanted to support Christopher in any way I could. I cooked, fed everyone and brought water. And I organized what he found. Christopher was unearthing and mourning the shards of his life, but the excavator had to keep going. I took each item out of his hands and kept it safe, so he could look at everything later. Some of us can do these things, some of us cannot. You couldn't carry out that service for him—but you could write about it!"

Kurt Boyer and Lew McMillan assisted Christopher over these weeks as well. Kurt attended almost all the excavations and photographed everything. Lew drove his Jeep down to the edge of the pit after work on many hot afternoons, in his white shirt and pith helmet, organized the gleanings into cardboard boxes and transported them to our RAV. Will Burt, Ruth's grandson, took time off work to help. Everyone smiled when an item emerged intact out of the mud and was held up for all to see.

Christopher returned to Kaslo late each evening, his eyes haunted. He'd crossed the River Styx and returned from Hades with physical proof and tales to tell of what exists beyond the grave. It sapped him; weight fell off him until he was a walking skeleton, with no buckle hole tight enough on his belt to hold up his pants.

Often palpably distressed when he opened the front door in the dying light, exhausted, ravenous and filthy, he still needed to first show me the latest collection of muddy treasures. Bags dripped. Boxes reeked of decomposition and mould, their unaccountable contents scabby with mud. Books were brick-like, hermetically sealed shut.

Christopher delivered his discoveries hesitantly, acutely attuned to my pain. He sometimes enquired first whether I'd have an interest in seeing a particular item he'd found. For instance, the delicate hand-knitted jacket that I'd laid out so proudly on the couch that last day. The glorious basket-weave creation was clotted with mud, stained and ripped. The beautiful aqua silk bouclé yarn had turned a rusty shade of green after four weeks' entombment. I spread the pitiful remnants on the front path, took a single photograph, and threw it all into the garbage.

I'd already mourned many of these things. I didn't nec-essarily want to be reminded of them again. But they re-emerged, like ghosts from our past life, and confronted me, some almost too poignant to bear. A torn "motivational" picture we'd jokingly taped on the wall at Ozzie's feeding station: a huge tiger's face above the word "Courage." Ozzie's comb, tins of cat food and a tiny fragment of his blue food dish.

I fingered the piece of dish. Every afternoon my darling cat started campaigning for his "tea" early in the afternoon. I'd tell him mock-sternly that his furry watch was Way Fast, and it was Much Too Early. But as soon as I put the kettle on for my own tea he knew it was time for his. He'd stretch up on his hind legs against the counter, front paws as high as the edge, talking, telling me to get a move on. We'd played this game together almost every day for eight years.

In short order we created what could only be described by the

uninitiated as abject chaos. Our cherished dwelling, cast in a ver-
dure of multi-hued greens and blooming flowers such a short time
before, was now a bomb crater set in a monochromatic battlefield.
Bits and scraps of our material lives lay scattered thick and at
random, decorating the mud walls of the crater.

Those close to him understood Christopher's need to excavate. But the idea of thrashing around in the muck and
mire of his past struck others as graceless, degrading and a
waste of time. Surely it would be kinder all round if he spared
himself (and others) the sight of this horror, left everything
buried and "moved on," as people glibly said.

Some visitors to the site, appalled at the mayhem, shook
their heads and asked, "Why on earth would you do this?"
The scene was so awful to behold that outsiders assumed it
must be awful for the victims too. But it wasn't that simple.

No outside observer can entirely understand what the
victims of such a disaster feel about it, or how they might respond. Is it perhaps the observer who wants to be spared the
ordeal of seeing the horror? Reburying the wreckage as fast
as possible (as was done, we learned later, on behalf of Lynn
Migdal, at the Webbers' house) was done as a "kindness," but
a kindness to whom?

For Christopher, the only imaginable response to his personal disaster was to go back and reclaim as much as possible
of his past. Why do we study history if not for the perspective it offers on present life? Why would Christopher leave
something in the ground, knowing he would never have the
resource to replace it? This was his personal archaeological
dig, with a visceral reward. It fed his need to take practical
action, and helped him deal with his grief. The articles he
recovered would be our companions from another life.

In Kaslo, I agonized over my uselessness. Christopher, in
the pit, had to decide on his own what to keep and what to
jettison. One afternoon I steeled myself and visited the site.

I drove up there alone, ready to turn tail and run if I had to. Christopher greeted me wearing a hard hat and a fluorescent safety vest. He grinned, upbeat and welcoming. He praised my bravery in coming, thanked me and showed me what he was up to that day.

At the sight of the pit I felt sick to my stomach. That earthy dank stink again. I could barely believe what I saw. Christopher was exhuming the corpse of our home, which had been tortured and rendered down to its elemental parts: fractured wood and pink insulation, twisted metal and cracked plastic, layered between mud and subjected to intense pressure. He pored over the inner organs, gristle and broken limbs, picking over bones, sifting through the fibres of our dwelling.

I tried to make sense of it. The scene resembled our local garbage dump before the introduction of steel containers. Except that I recognized every filthy rag, every shard of crockery and every broken shoe. Not garbage: our things. I noticed the red plastic fragments of my Samsonite suitcase— despite the manufacturers' guarantee, it was in fact very breakable. I gazed around the high earth walls of the tailings pile. Christopher had scooped out a ledge, a surreal earthen bookshelf, that displayed his Taschen art books on Van Gogh and Matisse. A well-trodden pathway wound around the side of the pit, strewn with boxes and half-empty water bottles.

Duncan had raised a piece of the kitchen floor. Underneath was the hanger rail, bolted to the basement ceiling, holding Christopher's shirts and pants. Most were still attached to their hangers. They'd slid along the ground, protected from above by the flooring. Some clothes were badly stained and torn but they'd sheltered others within what had become a fabric nest.

I spied Christopher's wedding shirt in the trash pile, ripped to pieces. A glint of light on one of the cuffs caught my eye. His grandfather's gold and diamond cufflinks, engraved with his initials, were still attached. I retrieved them, now wishing I'd been around more often to act as a second pair of eyes.

Out of his basement chest of drawers Christopher extracted folded shirts that had been compressed into wafers, rigid as cardboard. He retrieved quite a few clothes. Almost nothing survived from my closet and drawers upstairs in the bedroom.

MY MAJOR ROLE throughout August was dealing with muddy salvage. My cousin Melanie Klintworth flew from Vancouver for a short visit to offer her support. She was a great comfort—practical, down to earth, a rock. And she was family. I have a picture of her on our kitchen deck wielding a miniature broom she bought at the North Woven Broom Shop in Crawford Bay. The broom makers could never have imagined the use to which that tiny tool was put.

Melanie meticulously dusted the residue of dried mud and grit from every page of a particularly precious cookbook, *The Wooden Spoon Dessert Book*. We flicked the pages to prevent them sticking, and laid the book open on the deck, hoping the disinfectant qualities of sunshine would overpower the stink of mildew. We succeeded. Not our prettiest cookbook, but it lives on.

A neighbour passed by the Kaslo house and saw the copious laundry draped over the deck railing. "You need a clothesline," she informed me, and I agreed. Next thing I knew she was back with an umbrella-style clothes rack to sink into the ground. She said her name was Karen. I thanked her and told her my name.

"Yes, I know who you are," she said.

The washer churned all day. Clothing, bedding, towels and blankets. Sleeping bags and camping gear we laid out in the sun, but the cotton stuff-sacks had rotted to shreds in their time underground.

At least this disaster had happened at the height of summer. Days were long. Our meals were simple and easily prepared. We lived in T-shirts and shorts. I laid our laundry on the lawn, the fence, over bushes and in trees, for the entire world to see, and it was bone dry in a couple of hours.

Monday, August 27, the last day of excavation, was a twelve-hour marathon. Christopher left Kaslo at 5:30 a.m. Duncan started the machine at 7:00 a.m., and they worked non-stop, Christopher hobbling on crutches. He'd fractured a bone in his right foot about ten days earlier, but had paid it no heed for a week, until an X-ray showed the fracture and he was forced to attend to it.

Great things revealed themselves on the last day.

There is a slim, shiny, silver case now sitting next to the computer, about the size of a very svelte cigarette case. It contains the hard drive from Mandy's MacBook, "Macaroon." Looking at it, I see a hardened steel bucket half the size of this room, with the capacity to do in seven seconds what would take me two hours' hard labour. It crashes down and by casual association includes Macaroon in its jaw. Without laying into him with either molar or incisor it spins right, disgorges its mouthful and spins back for another massive bite.

Is that a glint of white I spy in the last load of rubble? I've been fooled a hundred times. Is it the afternoon sun clipping my glasses? My feet are rooted and it seems a long way away. My feet and eyes have been playing tricks on one another for days now—the diabolical reward for attempting to adjust to tri-focal progressives at precisely this point in time.

I put up my arm and the machine stops. I stumble across the distance. Between thumb and forefinger I pinch the radiused corner and pull it from the earth. After all the hours of following every theory imaginable as to the trajectory this little white MacBook could have followed, we finally find it in the counterintuitive upflow. I have it in my hands!

It's folded front to back as though to introduce a slight dihedral in a wing. The screen is a spider's web of fractured glass.

The touchpad is hanging by its tiny wire. Dried mud is jammed in every orifice but the four corners seem reasonably intact. Where in this compact box of marvels does the hard drive lie?

I have no time to luxuriate in such questions. I slide it into a box of crushed and muddied possessions. With spare words we agree on which corner to till next. The spectre of gargantuan machinery awaits. It has little patience. With a low growl it comes to life and we continue.

But the most important discovery of the entire excavation was still to come. The digger rototilled along the west side of the house in a final frenzied search for the elusive filing cabinet. The tailings pile grew into a towering mound of brown earth studded with pink insulation and splintered wood. Duncan stopped the machine for a moment to strategize with Christopher over the next move.

Christopher scanned the wall of freshly sifted soil. No! Surely not? Was that a smudge of black fur? He limped as fast as he could over to the tailings pile and gently lifted the small black corpse. He dropped to the ground, cradling Ozzie. Christopher, deeply absorbed in the task at hand, didn't usually allow himself any reaction to the finds, but this one was different. He let out a howl of anguish: "I've found my cat!"

Ozzie had indeed fled to his basement lair, high on a shelf, as we'd suspected. Christopher stroked the rough black fur, tears pouring down his face. Ozzie wasn't muddy or smelly. The only obvious injury on the limp body was a crushed skull, which meant he'd likely died instantly. Kurt put his hand on Christopher's shoulder. They placed the small body reverently into a box, where he lay until we could meet to bury him properly.

They did a bit more digging, but finding Ozzie extinguished the energy and clarity of focus. The beige filing cabinet was nowhere to be found. Christopher stood back and laid down his shovel. He called over to Duncan, "Just close it up." The giant bucket raked the debris back into the pit and filled it in with the pungent brown soil.

ON TUESDAY MORNING, August 28, 2012, Christopher, our niece Margie and I carried my MacBook with all due care and speed, like paramedics, to Greg, a computer guru Margie knew in upper Kaslo. A bear had invaded and ransacked his porch the previous night, and Greg performed brain surgery on Macaroon perched on a kitchen chair amidst the wreckage. It was all very Kootenay.

The hard drive slipped out, to be rehoused in its silver case. Greg gave me the connecting cords. Back home, I plugged it into my new computer. Up came the list: all my documents, including my previous book manuscript; 7,600 photographs; my email—everything! We'd done a séance, communicated with the dead, extracted a brain and Macaroon had loyally responded, after six weeks under the mud. Apple computers!

On Tuesday afternoon I wore a large hat. Christopher put on his favourite Hawaiian shirt, retrieved from under the mud. With Margie along, we drove to the Landing. Renata arrived by boat. Kurt joined us and we collected Ozzie's body. I held the box on my lap in the car. The weight felt right— the weight of my cat. But I was reluctant to look inside. How changed would he be?

We talked of Ozzie and remembered his endearing habits and sense of humour. How he'd learned to thump his tail against the window next to our bed—*thunk! thunk! thunk!*— at three a.m. when he wanted to come in. His evident distress if Christopher and I raised our voices in anger. His affection for us both, and expressions of delight when we got down on the floor for head-butting and nose-rubbing sessions. He understood the love talk we endlessly bestowed on him. He knew he was our *rey de la casa*. We'd been his devoted servants and we'd all loved every minute of it.

Christopher placed the box on the purple picnic table and opened it carefully, taking pains to protect me from the sight of his head injury. I concentrated my gaze on his black paws with their perfect leather pads and rounded claws. His paws were beautiful. The little cat was curled on his side as though in sleep. I stroked his back for the last time.

We'd brought a pillowcase shroud, and wrapped it and his body in an Irish linen tea towel that depicted a kitten. We took turns digging the hole under the mulberry tree in the garden, halfway between the graves of two other beloved felines: Renata's Kapiti and our first cat, Rocky. We marked Ozzie's grave with flat rocks specially chosen from the beach, and laid flowers on top.

Knowing where he rested was a comfort.

We next visited the new "mound," all that now remained of the spot where the house had stood. The bomb crater had vanished. Duncan had filled the hole and levelled it but the surface was rough and treacherous underfoot. He'd placed a large boulder on top of the mound, marking the approximate centre of the house. The boulder was comfortable to sit on.

Kurt, Renata, Margie, Christopher and I admired the breathtaking view down the lake, said our goodbyes to the house and gazed over this new and still alien landscape. The sun slipped towards the western ridge behind Lost Ledge. The light was soft and golden, anticipating fall. A gentle breeze ruffled our hair as we turned away and descended the hill, backlit by the setting sun.

Chapter 7: Counselling

CONFRONTING THE REMNANTS of our home, and previous lives, wasn't the only difficulty I faced in August. I lost my short-term memory and navigated in a dense fog. People addressed me and their words rolled like raindrops across my brain without sinking in. I was unable to absorb ideas, instructions or advice. Was I going mad? I watched myself in horror as I burst out in tantrums, shouted at my friends, dissolved in tears at the slightest provocation. Bad dreams haunted my nights until I was afraid to fall asleep. Thunderclaps or any sudden snapping noise triggered panic—my heart raced, I couldn't breathe and my limbs turned to jelly.

North Kootenay Lake Community Services runs its social programs from a quirky one-storey building with a faux turret roof, just around the block from our house. Millie Cumming took my initial contact call. Life was unbearable, I told her, and I didn't know what to do. I'd functioned pretty well at first, while we dealt with the practicalities, and while Christopher was with me for support. But when he was excavating in the Landing I was alone. Christopher and I seemed to be on divergent trajectories. I was wretched and afraid for our future.

MILLIE STOOPED TO light a yellow beeswax candle in a blue glass dish. She reminded me of a willow tree, supple, delicate. She moved lightly, with the precision of a ballet dancer. She wore her dark hair long, flowing in waves down her back. Straightening, she indicated a deep armchair, draped in a red blanket, which I sank into gratefully. I gazed around the small room. Books and cards stood on a shelf, posters and ropes of beads hung on the wall. Drawing paper, paints and crayons covered the table beside us. The light was subtly tinged greenish gold, diffused through the broad-fingered leaves of a huge maple tree outside the window. A peaceful room. Millie mentioned that she had specialist training in grief and trauma counselling.

"People grieve in different ways," she said after quietly listening to my concerns. Christopher, like many men, dealt with his loss through activity, in this case searching for salvage in the wreckage of our home. But my brain and body were warning me not to put myself in danger there again. Millie looked at me intently as I took in her words. If I acknowledged and honoured this reality, and allowed Christopher and myself space to grieve in our own ways, we would come back together again. This feeling of separation was a temporary stage in our ongoing journey.

I returned home from that first counselling session to find Christopher splayed out on the bed, exhausted. He'd locked the car keys inside the RAV in Johnson's Landing, and returned to Kaslo in Gail's truck to pick up the spare set. I lay down next to him and repeated what Millie had just told me. As I explained about our different ways of grieving, his face relaxed, and his body let go of tension. Relief and a new comprehension flooded through us. He drew me to him. We would get through this.

During another session, Millie asked about my immediate needs, as I perceived them. I had a list ready. I described feeling mentally scattered and manic, forgetful, thrashing around as though drowning. I needed a secure buoy to tie up to. I also wanted strength and confidence to face the next trip to England to see my mother, now re-booked for October. Right now I was incompetent. Attempts to concentrate, attend meetings or take in even simple instructions left me panic-stricken, overwhelmed and in tears. My third need—perhaps the most urgent one—was to feel safe again in the world.

Millie smiled. "This is normal," she said. "I know it's hard to understand. Your loss is like no one else's, but trauma affects us this way." If we dealt with it adequately now I would avoid post-traumatic stress disorder. "Would you be willing to try something?" I nodded. She offered me a basket of knitting yarns and I chose a ball of soft yellow mohair. I unwound the mohair to make a boundary around my chair until I was completely surrounded. Millie's voice intoned an incantation, encouraging me to feel completely safe here and now, inside my boundary. My manic thoughts dissolved into silence and I relaxed in the deep armchair, meditating on my breaths in and out. A deep calm infused my body, and lingered for the rest of the day. That night I drifted effortlessly into a good night's sleep.

Another day, Millie invited me to create a collage using words and pictures clipped from magazines. In half an hour I selected a small pile of snippets and quickly glued them onto a large sheet of paper. Each one knew its place. We stood back and considered the result.

In one corner I'd created a melancholy memorial for what was lost—Ozzie, the house, the garden. Another corner held menacing images of trees and mountains turned into agents of destruction. I'd placed a jaguar's big noble head, serene and regal, in the centre. He gazed into the far distance, as though to show me the long view of what Christopher and I still had: our lives, our relationship, our physical integrity and spiritual potential.

In the lower area of the collage I'd placed a picture of the Cathedral of Santiago de Compostela in Spain, thinking it signified the healing power of prayer and time. "I wonder if it holds a deeper wisdom," Millie said.

I had a particular connection to that cathedral. Just before writing up my Ph.D. thesis at Bristol University in 1984, I decided to make a pilgrimage with a friend by bicycle to Santiago de Compostela. Starting in the south of France, we crossed the Pyrenees and travelled west along the ancient Way of St. James, as pilgrims have been doing since the eleventh century. We arrived in Santiago at the beginning of Easter Week—Semana Santa.

I told Millie about the Baroque façade of the cathedral, erected in the eighteenth century, directly in front of the medieval Pórtico de la Gloria of 1188. That April afternoon in 1984, a blustery day under rain-sodden grey clouds, I climbed the steep stone steps from the square, euphoric to have completed my pilgrimage. Entering through the great Baroque doorway, the Pórtico de la Gloria quietly greeted me in partial shadow. Eyes adjusting to the gloom, I made out the naturalistic, intensely compassionate, peaceful statue of St. James that welcomes pilgrims with a gentle smile and benediction. The central entrance pillar depicts the Tree of Jesse, and I placed the five fingers of my right hand into five deep sockets in the stone, worn away by the touch of millions of pilgrims. I was just one more such pilgrim, carried to that spot by historical continuity, shared intention and the stream of life.

Thanks to the cathedral's ugly Baroque façade, the beautiful Pórtico de la Gloria is protected from weather damage and even has some of its original paint intact—a hidden gift to each pilgrim who climbs the steps and enters through the great doorway at the end of their gruelling journey.

Millie watched as I told the story. When I stopped she cocked her head as though waiting for me to grasp a new concept.

Did the landslide hold a hidden gift like that for me? Could something positive emerge from under the mud, out of all that horror and destruction?

AT A SESSION in mid-August, Millie invited me to draw something. Instantly apprehensive, I tried to say no, then made some half-hearted squiggles on the paper. Hopeless! I skewered holes in the paper with the pencil and rummaged for a Kleenex, my eyes overflowing with tears of frustration and regret. Why bother? I couldn't do art any more. Miserably, I told Millie about the delight I used to derive from pen and ink sketching and watercolour painting.

But ten years before the slide it all dried up; both artist's and writer's block paralyzed me. I had no idea why it happened, but losing my powers of creative self-expression had been a quiet, personal tragedy I tried not to think about.

Yet now, here I was in Kaslo, writing non-stop! It was all I could do to save my sanity. The experience of breaking open and writing everything down was like coming unstuck; the landslide had swept me forward.

When Christopher returned that night, muddy and weary, I poured us each a beer and we sat on the kitchen deck to quietly contemplate and comment on our day. "I wonder," I began tentatively, "if I needed this change. There are certainly more opportunities for me here in Kaslo."

Christopher rested his head against the wall and said he was glad Millie and I were exploring these big questions. He thought it would be a helpful grounding for us as we went forward. And that he had no doubt that our relationship would endure, stronger and perhaps healthier, if we each followed the passion that fed our soul. Our new paths would weave together. We'd find a way to do it.

MILLIE LISTENED SYMPATHETICALLY as I talked about my mother. I hadn't told my mother about our ordeals, and the nursing home staff advised me not to upset her. I phoned one day, and waited while they transferred my call, wondering how I'd keep up the pretence that everything was normal. But it was easy. June was oblivious to my presence or absence that particular day and seemed unaware that I was in Canada.

Even so, to remain silent was enormously difficult for the child in me and I grappled with a huge sense of loss. Even with dementia, my mother loved me unconditionally and had always expressed her affection so sweetly and demonstrably. I was the most cherished person in her world. She wanted to know about the slightest sniffle, minor accident or mishap I might suffer, and would try to kiss everything better and set my world right.

But this time I could not run to her for solace. I donned a mask and kept secret from my mother the most traumatic catastrophe that had ever befallen her beloved daughter.

I told Millie about the day recently when I'd phoned June and found her unusually lucid. She asked after Christopher, then Ozzie. I didn't tell her that Christopher was mourning our lost home, or that Ozzie's skull had been crushed. No. I steeled myself, took a deep breath and said, "He's fine, we're all fine," as I visualized the small body quietly decomposing in its grave beside the mulberry tree. My mother enquired several times as to how old Ozzie now was and I said, "He's nine."

Time and aging stopped for him that day and he'll always be nine.

I couldn't tell her the truth. Her short-term memory non-existent, the news would have bewildered her. She'd have been agitated and alarmed but then forgotten why she was upset. My explanations would have sunk like stones to the murky depths of her mind. The ripples of comprehension would still themselves and we'd be back where we started. She'd ask after Christopher, and then Ozzie, and I'd tell her they were both "fine."

AFTER EIGHT WEEKS of counselling I began to find my courage again. I stood back, mentally, and tried to reflect objectively on the previous nineteen years of my life, beginning with the moment we'd arrived at our new home in the Landing, one snowy evening in December 1993. We slid back the bar on the curious Dutch-style door of Ruth's house, stepped inside, sniffed the perfume of old cedar and fell under its spell, bewitched and enchanted. We loved it unconditionally, called it our paradise, and hated to leave. The house embraced us. It would never let us go.

The house held great promise of eventual perfection, but required boundless energy and commitment, and we never quite kept up with its demands. The three-year roof project, for instance, an enormous undertaking, nearing completion that summer of 2012, had taken hundreds of hours of devoted labour.

Christopher redesigned the roof, extended it over the deck, increased the insulative thickness, translated calculations into wood cuts, sought materials, prepped, stained, fitted the wood, reinsulated and sheathed it with plywood, and then we finally put down the membrane layer. We stuck down the last strip of membrane at the end of October 2011 just as temperatures were plummeting. The membrane saw us through that final winter, but it leaked. Always we'd have these tussles of will between materials and the elements.

But I remember my delight, standing on the roof, at treetop level, surveying the breathtaking views of the yard and creek, and the lake glittering through the fir trees beyond. We vowed to put a proper roof terrace up there eventually, once all the other jobs were done.

The longer the projects sat unfinished the harder it became to re-engage with them. They gathered cobwebs and lurked reproachfully. I think it sapped Christopher's spirit. A meticulous perfectionist, he worked all the time. I rarely saw him sit down to indulge his love of reading or enjoy the view. He tended to take on too much, and I worried about the strain it put him under.

I joked about living in a building site, but it was sometimes a point of friction. Alone, I ranted to the heavens, hating the unfinished walls, the tuck tape and vapour barrier, our bed stuck in the living room. If it hadn't been such a glorious space to wake up in, I might have made more fuss. And secretly I envied friends who lived in finished houses, but if I raised the subject Christopher was instantly defensive: "Why don't you help me more? I've told you all the things you could be doing." I yearned to feel enthusiasm for the construction projects that surrounded us, but my heart wasn't in it. I didn't want us to spend all our time working on the house.

After the landslide, after that terrible annihilation, only then was the spell of the enchanting house broken, for me at least. We never would have wanted such a thing to happen, but in a moment the projects were swept away, gone forever. I could let them go relatively easily, but Christopher was invested, heart and soul, in all those improvements and the vision of perfection they promised. He lost a great deal more than I did.

THREE MONTHS AFTER the landslides I noticed the glimmerings of my old sense of humour. I emailed a photo to some friends in England of Christopher and me standing together on the rough mound of soil that covers the house. All the glory of Kootenay Lake stretches away behind us, bathed in the golden light of a late summer evening. My caption in the email read: "Two old survivors stand on the site of their former home. The view is even more stunning now all those pesky trees are gone!"

My friend Jules responded with a verse by a seventeenth-century Japanese poet, Mizuta Masahide, who wrote in a similarly ironic vein: "Barn's burnt down—now I can see the moon."

ABOUT A MONTH after the slides our niece Margie moved into our spare bedroom and stayed until September. She and Lila had done all they could for Lynn Migdal, who returned to Florida in early August.

We've known Margie since she was a chubby toddler crawling among the lush vegetable beds in her parents' garden at Harvey's pottery house, her bright eyes missing no detail of bug and flower. She was a child of Johnson's Landing for eight of her first thirteen years.

Then the family moved away to Kaslo and we watched Margie growing up from a distance. Of course we got together for family meals and celebrations but, having no children of my own, I felt shy in her presence, uncertain of what to say or how to relate. I must have seemed distant, aloof and very old. Now Margie was almost twenty-two—mature for her age, and made older by the horrors she'd witnessed and her exposure to grief.

Margie and I enjoyed good times during August and September. We'd share a glass of red wine or a whisky and ginger on the little kitchen deck in the cool of the evening. Margie was fun, good company, and cheered me up when Christopher was away. She took over all kitchen duties and cooked up delicious gourmet meals, using the freshest organic produce from her dad's garden in upper Kaslo.

Margie was in mourning over Diana's death, and she sometimes turned inward, escaping her sorrows within the covers of a book. She reread the entire seven-volume Harry Potter series while she was with us. One day I asked what she missed most about Diana. After a pause she said, "I miss talking to her; our conversations on so many different topics. We discovered so much together. I often find myself thinking, Diana would understand this, but I know nobody else is going to quite get it."

When Christopher and I felt weak, Margie was strong. We hugged and cried together. We grew to know one another and I was immensely grateful to have her as a member of my family. At the end of September she presented us with a farewell card she'd bought in Vancouver just three days before the landslide. Like her dream, it held elements of premonition. I read it several times in amazement. The picture shows a lady rabbit being serenaded by a handsome male rabbit dressed in a red cape. She announces to him:

You can't ultimately safe-guard anything in this world;
anything can be lost, destroyed or taken away.
Seeking only possessions and status leads to worry and sorrow.

Her suitor replies:

I don't care. I'm keeping the cape.

The card had struck Margie as poignant, she told us, but she had no inkling of the significance those words would come to hold.

I WAS ONE of Millie's last Kaslo clients. She broke the news to me that she'd be leaving her job at the end of September. At first I baulked. I needed her wisdom and had come to depend on our regular meetings; I wasn't ready to go forward on my own. But Millie assured me I was doing well. The best therapy was the one I'd developed for myself—writing everything down, telling my story and plumbing its depths.

At the end of our last session together Millie wished me well and extinguished the beeswax candle. I owe Millie a huge debt of gratitude for everything she did to assist me in my recovery.

I began to look outward, beyond my own personal story, and wondered about our friends and neighbours in the Landing. What had happened to everyone else over those terrible days in July? And subsequently? Christopher and I had been cast adrift. In the first stage of post-trauma I was completely self-centred in my grief and needs. I might have realized vaguely that of course we were not the only ones affected by this disaster, but like many survivors of a traumatic event, I was not in my right mind for many months.

Gradually, the extent and magnitude of the catastrophe began to dawn on me. My curiosity rekindled, I wanted to know about everyone else. I sat down and drew up a list of people to talk to: thirty-five names. I wondered how it would be to ask if they'd allow me to interview them, and try to capture the larger story.

When I asked people if I might record an interview about their experiences, the response was overwhelmingly positive. Friends and neighbours from the Landing visited me in Kaslo, sat down at our sunny dining table, and gave their time generously. I visited others in their homes and conducted some interviews over the phone. Diffident and tongue-tied at first, I became more confident as the collection of interviews grew, and developed a simple template of questions. How did you discover the Landing originally? Why did you move there? Where were you on July 12 and what happened? How are you feeling now, all these months later?

I extended my interview list to include members of the emergency response team, the Red Cross, RCMP, friends of the victims, journalists. Almost without exception people agreed to talk to me and seemed glad—indeed relieved—to do so.

They thanked me for what I was doing. They felt comfortable, they said, telling me their stories, and appreciated my doing this important work for our collective community memory. Listening to their often sad and emotional recollections I was like a priest in the confessional. And they trusted me. I'd not expected that. I recorded our interviews, typed up the stories, conferred and corrected the text. Then, for my own well-being, I tried to let each story go. My book would be our permanent repository.

Chapter 8: Those Who Were There

THURSDAY, JULY 12, 2012, was a hot, cloudless day. "We're going to the beach!" Rachel Rozzoni exclaimed on the phone to a friend when she saw the brilliant blue sky that morning. A day for visiting neighbours and taking things easy, thought Bob Yetter, who'd had heart surgery recently. Early-rising country folk like John Madill and Harvey Armstrong had already completed a full day's work before 10:30 a.m., shovelling gravel, cutting hay and making firewood. Others arose late and prepared large breakfasts in celebration of this stunningly beautiful vacation day at the height of midsummer.

Petra Frehse

No one can know exactly what Petra Frehse did that morning, but from the facts told to me by others, along with her habits and routines, her morning might have transpired something like this:

Petra probably smiled to herself as she sipped her morning coffee and inhaled deeply on a cigarette. She'd said that the first coffee and cigarette of the day were always the best. She drew back the red and white checked curtains and looked out the kitchen window. Her special deer were there as usual, tame as could be, a doe with two fawns, feeding contentedly on the scraps she'd put on the lawn for them. The creek was thundering down the hill beyond the garden, louder than ever. Petra's mother, Ruth Vogt, called daily from her home in the Black Forest of Germany, to check that everything was all right. On Wednesday Petra had told her how shocked she'd been to see the horrible colour of the creek—as black as her coffee.

She'd also said that she hadn't seen a bear in the yard yet this year. Bears were Petra's passion. Her small, orderly living room was filled to the rafters with stuffed teddy bears, mostly her own handmade white spirit bears. A huge brown teddy bear, larger than Petra, sat in a chair near the dining table, taking up much of the room.

The phone rang, as it did every morning, at around ten a.m. Her mother worried terribly. Eighty-six years old and in frail health, Ruth would have preferred that Petra didn't spend half the year in Canada. But Petra had said many times that Johnson's Landing was her soul-home, the only place she wanted to be.

Petra and her husband, Jürgen Frehse, bought their property in Johnson's Landing in 1989 after searching across North America for the perfect place. They fell in love with the 1930s heritage cabin tucked into a grassy glade beside Gar Creek.

After Jürgen died in 2006, Petra retired from her job with a German broadcasting company and began spending six months of the year in the Landing. She hated having to return to Germany and would telephone Jillian Madill every Sunday during those dark, absent months while she counted the days until spring, when she'd board the plane in Frankfurt and return to her *real* home, in the Kootenays.

As part of Petra's routine, every Thursday she drove to Argenta to have morning coffee with her good friend Edith Mautner. Edith, in her late nineties, was Petra's Canadian "mom" and they greatly enjoyed these weekly get-togethers. But this week Edith had a medical appointment on Thursday, so Petra had visited her on Tuesday instead.

On Thursday Petra's last words to her mother were, "Now I'll go and make myself a good cup of coffee, but not with this awful coffee-brown creek water."

Lila Taylor

Lila was cooking breakfast in the gleaming wooden kitchen of her parents' timber-frame house. It stood like an eagle's nest among the fir trees, overlooking Kootenay Lake. The kitchen window faced the ravine and Lila could hear the creek pounding below the house. At around 10:20 the phone rang—Diana Webber was on the line, at home with her dad and sister on the other side of the creek.

Diana sounded strange, unsettled and anxious. Something was wrong, she told Lila, and she wanted to get out of her dad's house as soon as possible. Lila was surprised. Normally the Webbers' place was their hangout spot. Lila invited Diana to join her right then for breakfast, but Diana declined. Her dad was cooking breakfast for his girls, so she'd eat at home with Val and Rachel, then drive over to Lila's afterwards, in about twenty minutes' time.

They hung up and Lila sat down to breakfast with her family. Her father, Richard Taylor, is a well-known and highly regarded local artist, and her mother, Susan Grimble, is a Feldenkrais practitioner. Richard's two young granddaughters were also with them, visiting from California.

When they heard the booming noise, Lila and her parents raced outside and watched in disbelief as part of the landslide roared down the ravine below their house like a low-flying jet plane, snapping off trees in its path. Lila's first thought was, "This'll be a fun day for me and Diana, but we'll probably be stuck on opposite sides of the creek." It took the family a few moments to register another significant thought: *Mandy and Christopher's house!*

Loran Godbe

Loran didn't get to bed until past daybreak. From his home, the highest house in the Landing, he'd monitored the creek's bizarre behaviour throughout Wednesday, and sent his second email advisory to everyone in the community at around five a.m. on Thursday morning.

Loran described sudden surges of dark water, each of which brought down more logs and woody debris. Gravel deposits and a nearby logjam had obliterated the community water intake. The driveway was impassable—the culvert was so clogged with debris that virtually the entire creek was flowing over and along it in raging flood.

His email continued:

> The entire creek bed is raw and constantly being scoured and re-shaped. Mom and I sat for an hour on our trail just above the creek and watched… Within ten minutes, in any given spot, the creek bed might be filled in [with gravel]… then the water would change course and it would be scoured out again. We heard large rocks banging along the creek bed underwater.

At 10:30 a.m. Loran and his mother, Linda, were asleep in the house they share with Gerry Rogers on the north hillside overlooking Gar Creek. Gerry had risen early as usual, and left home at around 10:00 a.m. He forded the creek at a spot some distance above their treacherous driveway, and went to tend to their horse, which was stabled near the Johnson's Landing Retreat Centre.

Loran woke to a sound, and knew instantly what it was. He has no idea how he got from his bed, out through the door and to the lawn so quickly. The slide—he knew he was looking at a slide—was approximately opposite the house, about fifty metres away, thundering down the creek. Loran estimates it was moving at close to 160 kilometres an hour.

A hurricane-force wind that pushed ahead of the slide blasted the trees horizontal and snapped their tops off. The ear-splitting noise—a low-frequency rumble caused by the crashing rocks and trees, and a high-pitched scream like a jet engine from the wind—was so loud Loran thought his hearing could be damaged. The air was filled with dust and resin from exploding trees. For more than an hour afterwards he and Linda couldn't breathe outside without a mask.

The ground was shaking as though a freight train was passing by. Indoors, Linda had leapt out of bed and stood in the middle of the living room. The house was quaking, their kiwi vine outside the window vibrating; she was convinced that the landslide was already surging around the house foundations and there was no escape. She stood rooted to the spot, expecting the house to collapse. She believed she was about to die.

Loran followed the sound as the slide carried on down the hill, heading for the lake. In his interview he told me his first thought was, "Oh my God! There go Christopher and Mandy! My heart sank and I could hardly breathe. I knew it was the end for you guys." Indoors, Linda's first words were also, "Oh no! Christopher and Mandy!" Loran was shaking so badly he could barely walk, not so much from fear as from the magnitude of the experience. He'd been so close to the visceral power of the low frequencies, they seemed to have affected his nervous system. His body shook for minutes afterwards.

Boulders continued falling into the creek and trees burst from the strain of being bent over. After that it was eerily silent.

John Madill

John and Jillian's gracious log house stood at the top of Holmgren Road, a hundred metres below the Godbe–Rogers driveway, and adjacent to Petra Frehse's property.

I often stopped to watch Gar Creek from the driveway bridge. The water gushed under the horizontal root of an old cedar stump and chattered onward between mossy boulders, down to the lake. Wild blackcurrant bushes nodded on the bank.

This was our paradise, a rustic Kootenay house beside the lake; shady in summer, protected in winter, with a million-dollar view. It's shown here in the fall of 2010 as Virginia creeper turned red and the roof was under reconstruction.

Driftwood and iris under Ruth's cypress tree made a welcoming garden on our driveway south of Gar Creek. Some iris survived but the cypress tree was felled by the slide.

The post office cabin is a one-room log house dating from the 1920s that had served as the community's post office in the early days of settlement. It has accommodated many passing travellers and visitors over the years.

Our garden became a study in driftwood and rock decoration. The gateposts were two upended driftwood tree trunks, their root balls standing tall like hairy headed giants. Driftwood created the gate, wove along the fence and marked out the garden beds.

A short path led from the driveway down to Johnson's Landing's beach and the bay that looks south towards Birchdale, Kaslo and beyond. Christopher constructed a boardwalk and deck so our friend, Paul Hunter, could join us there in his wheelchair.

[ABOVE] The first landslide left Gar Creek brim-full of trees and mud. Only about half the debris descended the creek channel.

[LEFT] The first debris flow in the channel on July 12, ground to a halt at the mouth of Gar Creek, depositing very little into the lake. Our roof is visible on the left edge of the slide, near the shoreline.

The house was pushed, folded diagonally and collapsed. Windows blew out,
walls flipped over but the movement was so gentle that pots of herbs
and geraniums still clung to the edge of the deck.

The roof crashed onto the deck and the corner post snapped;
the landslide pushed the house about three metres towards the lake.

The morning following the first slide I returned to our homesite in a friend's boat. After an ear-splitting cracking noise exploded above us we raced back to the boat and sped away from shore, chased by the second slide. We watched as the creek disgorged its innards and the house disappeared under waves of mud.

The second slide scoured out the creek channel, depositing 10,000 cubic metres of tree debris into the lake.

The path of the landslide: approximately 320,000 cubic metres of soil and rock
travelled at speeds of up to 150 kilometres per hour down the Gar Creek channel.
Half the material leapt out of the channel and poured across the Johnson's Landing
bench, destroying three homes and killing four people.

PHOTO: CHRISTOPHER KLASSEN

The home of John and Jillian Madill was caught by the edge of the slide. John sprinted clear, behind the wall on the left side of this photo, but was pelted by flying debris. A log skewered the house from front to back.

PHOTO: COURTESY BC MINISTRY OF TRANSPORTATION AND INFRASTRUCTURE

This photo shows the slide path viewed from the source area.
The total distance to the lake is 2.8 kilometres.

The vast wave of material buried the Webbers' house. It side-swiped Harvey Armstrong's pottery studio and house, causing substantial damage.

Our driveway and garden were inundated by silt after the second landslide.

Vancouver's Heavy Urban Search and Rescue (HUSAR) task force
deployed to Johnson's Landing within twenty-hour hours.

HUSAR provided personnel and equipment but task force members were unfamiliar
with the lay of the land and the exact location of the Webber and Frehse house sites.

Neighbour Bob Yetter drew a diagram of the Webber house orientation and its relation
to existing landmarks in order to assist HUSAR members in their search.

Facing an incredibly difficult and dangerous job, the bravery
and commitment of all the rescue teams was admirable.

One week after the landslides, this was my first sight of our home: an earthy mound, some bunched timbers, an edging of deck and a bit of roof held against two brave old fir trees that had somehow stood strong.

Christopher, Roger, Carol and Kurt sat down at our mauve picnic table. I took a photo of my four shell-shocked companions in front of what looked like a movie set from a dystopian film. They looked like ghosts. I don't know how we could even eat, talk or walk.

Derek Baker brought his barge to Johnson's Landing on Sunday, July 15.
He made numerous trips across the lake ferrying stranded vehicles
to the highway at Schroeder Creek.

Duncan Lake and his excavator uncover 'Jerald' our Toyota Tercel
within an hour of the first day of excavation at the house-site.

Christopher laboured in the pit, exhuming the corpse of our home.

"I was left alone under a blue sky, puffs of white cloud, the expanse and satisfaction of Kootenay Lake laid out before me to both north and south. The meditative quiet was broken only by the thud and clink of my pick and shovel as I probed yet another corner of hell."
—Christopher Klassen

Christopher stands amidst a scene resembling a garbage dump. Except that we recognized every filthy rag, shard of crockery and broken shoe. Not garbage: our things.

RCMP Corporal Chris Backus (shown here with his dog Caesar) arrived at Gar Creek within two hours of the first slide and stayed in the Landing for a week. Residents noted that "he went way above and beyond the call of duty."

As the incident commander and rescue mission coordinator, Kaslo Search and Rescue manager Bruce Walker also provided assistance to the Vancouver HUSAR team.

Excavator operator Duncan Lake assisted many people with hazardous digging projects beside and within the Gar Creek channel.

Deb Borsos, North Kootenay Lake's emergency contact person, became the Regional District of Central Kootenay's recovery manager for the Johnson's Landing disaster.

Retired coroner and forensic anthropology specialist Bob Stair conducted the recovery operation on behalf of the BC Coroners Service. After Val and Diana Webber's bodies were found, BC's chief coroner suspended the recovery operation. Bob persuaded her to authorize a resumption of the search a week later, and recovered Rachel Webber's body on July 25.

Petra Frehse—her cabin was located beside the creek with windows overlooking an untamed garden and the wildlife she adored. Misinformation about her whereabouts prior to the slide delayed the search of the site near her own home.

A memorial rock and plaque stand on the small remaining corner of Petra Frehse's land in Johnson's Landing.

Valentine Webber loved to be on the lake in his dark green wooden rowboat, the *Diana K.*

Val Webber and his girls, Diana and Rachel, were having breakfast
together in their home when the slide occurred.

Only minutes before the landslide and feeling inexplicably unsettled, Diana Webber
phoned a friend and arranged to visit her on the other side of the creek
after finishing breakfast with her dad and sister.

In the days after the tragedy Val Webber's kindly smiling face gazed out
from the front pages of national newspapers, his arm embracing Rachel,
one of his two beloved daughters.

Rachel Webber—when the chief coroner warned that she might never be located in the massive debris field, some of Rachel's young friends refused to accept the prospect of not recovering her and vowed to go to Johnson's Landing and dig with their own hands.

Diana had driven up from Los Angeles and spent a couple of days in Kaslo visiting her sister Rachel. On the day before the landslide, Diana and Rachel drove to the Landing so they could spend time together with their dad.

[Left to right] Diana and Rachel's mother, Lynn Migdal, and friends Lila Taylor and Margie Smith in Val's rowboat on the first anniversary of the landslide, July 12, 2013.

On the first anniversary, Renata Klassen scatters petals on the water in memory of the four who died.

PHOTO: MARGARET SMITH

Two old survivors: Mandy Bath and Christopher Klassen, stand on the earthy mound, site of their former home.

PHOTO: LYNNE CAMPBELL

The driveway and abandoned garden are still beautiful in October 2014.

John said goodbye to Jillian just before nine o'clock Thursday morning, and she drove off down the road in the silver Buick to meet me at Creek Corner.

At 10:30 a.m. John, in his coveralls, was behind the garage and guesthouse, seventy-five metres from the house, collecting gravel and small stones for a building project. He loved to putter around the homestead, never short of jobs to do. He shovelled the gravel into a trailer attached to his ATV—strenuous work, and a heavy load to pull. He climbed onto the ATV and trundled slowly back towards the house, admiring the colourful perennials and the vibrant young corn plants, taller by the day, standing in their dark green rows.

John had just reached the house and climbed off his ATV when he heard rocks and scree tumbling down in the ravine. His instinct was to bolt in the opposite direction, back along the driveway towards the guesthouse. Then he heard a much louder noise: a rumbling roar, accompanied by a powerful downdraft of wind that flattened the trees. He had the presence of mind and just enough time to turn back to the house and sprint behind the west wall. The slide thundered past, higher than the house, burying the driveway, the garden, the garage and the guesthouse, plus their vehicles, camper and boat. A tree pierced the house, narrowly missing him. Flying debris hit him in the face.

Jillian said later, "John thinks clearly in a crisis and makes cool-headed decisions. I believe it was that trait that saved his life." He is also very fit and agile for his age. Afterwards he found it difficult to talk about his incredible escape. "It was like a tornado with stuff flying through the air. The wind and the noise were terrible. I wouldn't want to go through something like that ever again."

When the noise stopped, John's first thought was for their cat, Tumbles, but the cat was nowhere to be seen. The house was a wreck, punctured by enormous trees, but the main debris flow had missed the building by centimetres. John grabbed his air horn and climbed the hill in search of Petra.

He couldn't believe his eyes: there was only a small triangle of original ground left. Her house, carport and shed had disappeared under metres of wet mud, laced with boulders and trees. He sounded his air horn.

Bob Yetter and Harvey Armstrong

Down the hill from the Madills' property, Bob and Susan's circular, hand-built timber-frame house nestles into the hillside on a knoll of land, looking out over a sweeping view southward down Kootenay Lake. They moved from Montana to the Landing in 1999, bought their land in 2001, built a workshop, then the house, and finally took up residence there in 2008.

Bob Yetter, a woodsman and carpenter, was alone that morning. His wife, Susan VanRooy, a nature journalist and watercolour artist, had left the previous day to travel with her parents to a family reunion in Ontario. Bob was recovering from heart surgery; he'd had a stent fitted at the end of May and was taking life a little easier. He'd resolved to make some changes on account of "the heart thing"; he wanted to get out to spend more time with his neighbours. Around 10:30 a.m., hearing the sound of Harvey Armstrong's chainsaw, Bob went outside and ambled up the hill for a chat.

Harvey was also alone that day. His wife, Kate O'Keefe, had left early and driven to Kaslo, picked up Osa Thatcher and continued on to Nelson to attend a watercolour workshop. Harvey had been busy that morning cutting grass for hay in their large meadow, south of Kootenay Joe Farm. He and Kate lived in Algot Johnson's original log house, beautifully restored and enlarged. Harvey also owned the four-hectare property next to the Madills, uphill from Bob and Susan's land. It was home to his pottery buildings, a rental house (where our niece Margie had lived as a child) and his woodlot, where he was now hard at work dicing up rounds of lodgepole pine. It was a hot morning and he appreciated the shady canopy of trees overhead.

Bob and Harvey exchanged only a few sentences of conversation before they heard the noise. "Wait. Listen. What's that?" said Bob. "A truck on the road? No, that's *in* the creek. That's something big." As the noise rose to a crescendo Bob yelled, *"Run!"* and they dashed to a ridge about 140 metres away from the creek, near Bob and Susan's house. They stopped running only because the noise immediately above them also stopped.

Looking towards Gar Creek, Bob watched the slide's transit down the channel, marked by the trees toppling in its path. That last phase of the slide went past in about five seconds. He knew our house must have been hit. He shot indoors and called 911, becoming the first person to do so, then he and Harvey drove to Creek Corner, where the road now ended, and sprinted down the hill.

Rachel Rozzoni

Rachel Rozzoni, a mother and homesteader in her late thirties, stood in the kitchen of her house on Holmgren Road, almost opposite the Webbers' property. Her older children, Aidan and Giselle, ages fifteen and thirteen, were still asleep upstairs.

Rachel and her husband, Dan Tarini, had moved the family to the Landing nine years earlier, greatly attracted by "that beautiful place under the mountain," with its sun exposure, lack of mosquitoes and fabulous views. They set up a small farming operation, and raised goats and purebred Labrador puppies to pay the bills. Rachel sold goat's milk, yoghurt and cheese.

Dan and Rachel had separated and she and her new partner, Riki, had an eight-month-old baby girl, Avalia. Spring 2012 had felt full of promise. Rachel and Giselle worked together in the garden from April till early July preparing the beds, replanting strawberries, hand-watering plant starts and running around in their bare feet, feeling happy and connected to the land. Baby Avalia played in the dirt.

Thursday, July 12, was one of those perfect summer days with a crystal clear blue sky. Rachel phoned a friend in Argenta and made plans to take the kids on a picnic. At 10:37 she was standing in the kitchen, contemplating what to take for the picnic, when Avalia suddenly looked up from the floor where she was learning to crawl, uttered an uncharacteristic shriek of pure distress and reached up for her mother, trembling.

Rachel picked Avalia up from the kitchen floor, wondering what was wrong, until she too felt the vibration; the whole house shook. Cups bounced on the table. Rachel's first thought was war—a war had started and a hundred helicopters were rattling overhead. She ran outside onto the deck, scanned the sky and peered into the woods. Nothing seemed amiss but the noise was now deafening. She returned to the kitchen window.

Through the forest a vast wave of earth was coming straight for her like a bulldozer, mowing down trees in its path. They were going to die. It was going to cover the house. She held her baby tight. But at the last moment a slight swale in the ground diverted the mountain of material and it swept across their driveway and Holmgren Road, crashing down over Val Webber's house instead. Rachel heard a sharp *snap* as the power and phone lines were ripped off her house.

Then there was silence, apart from the voice screaming in Rachel's head: "Val's house! Oh my God, we've got to go and help them." Aidan and Giselle rushed downstairs. Riki appeared from the basement. There was instant chaos. They needed to get out fast; everyone needed shoes; the baby was naked. They tumbled out the door and ran towards the Webbers' house, then stopped dead in their tracks. The roof was floating in a sea of gravelly mud in completely the wrong place. Trees and boulders lay everywhere.

No hope. No hope for them. There was no question in Rachel's mind.

Renata Klassen

Down at the post office cabin beside our garden, Renata had unpacked her belongings and settled in. After his strenuous early morning walk, Lennie, her elderly golden retriever, had passed out on the cool cabin floor. Ren and I checked our improvised sand-bagging on the creek bank. I'd picked peonies and foxgloves and put them in a vase on the mauve picnic table.

Renata said goodbye to me at around 8:45. She wanted to do a load of laundry in the basement at our house but kept putting it off. At 10:35 she decided to empty the food scraps out of her bucket onto the compost heap in the garden. After that she'd grab the clothes hamper and stroll up the driveway, over the bridge to our place.

Renata was walking back from the compost heap when she heard a noise like boulders rolling down the mountain. It seemed to emanate from high on the bench of land above the beach. She roused Lennie from the cabin floor. At first she fled from the sound, up the driveway towards our house, but when she reached the iris bed just before the storage shed she realized she'd made a terrible mistake. The slide snapped and crashed down the creek towards her, the noise excruciating. She shouted to her dog, "Come on, Lennie! Turn around! Let's go! Let's go!" and hurtled back towards the garden. Her legs turned to rubber, she couldn't take another step. She peed her pants. The slide roared across the driveway behind her. Everything stopped.

"It was the most earth-shattering, terrifying, life-altering thing I ever expect to experience," she told me later. The next few minutes were surreal. Renata stood in the driveway with Lennie; to the right lay our garden: lush and normal. To the left, the driveway abruptly ended in a wall over a storey high of brown mud and trees without limbs or bark, denuded. The house was gone. There was silence, and then the birds began to sing again.

Richard Ortega, Gerry Rogers and Roger

At the top of Kootenay Joe Road, Richard Ortega and Gerry Rogers (still on his way to visit the horse) stood outside the Johnson's Landing Retreat Centre in deep discussion with a young man named Kyle, the Corix installation engineer, who'd turned up that morning in his truck. Neither Kootenay Joe Farm nor the Retreat Centre had permitted him to replace their electricity meters with smart meters, so he planned to try his luck farther up Holmgren Road at the Frehse, Madill and Webber residences. Just as soon as he got done with this rather intense conversation on the ethics of smart meters.

Roger drove up Kootenay Joe Road pulling his trailer, saw the Corix truck parked outside the Retreat Centre and swore under his breath. *Damn it! They'd finally arrived.* He carefully negotiated a U-turn with the trailer in tow and returned to the house he shared with Carol on the north side of the creek. Carol immediately put up a sign beside their electricity meter; they wanted nothing to do with smart meters in that household.

Roger swung out of their driveway again and crossed Gar Creek for the third time in twenty minutes—he was one of the last to see the old Creek Corner intact. The water looked even thicker and blacker this morning, and he felt vaguely uneasy due to the intensely earthy, rank, swampy smell. What the hell was going on? Thank goodness he'd pulled his backhoe out of the creek draw the day before.

Back on Kootenay Joe Road, Roger briefly joined Gerry and Richard and added his two cents' worth to the discussion with Kyle, but he had work to do and abandoned the conversation to get on with the business of loading a large log onto his trailer.

Driving back down Kootenay Joe Road a few minutes later, Roger heard strange banging and crashing noises. Was something wrong with his load? The log not strapped down properly? A problem with his trailer? Jesse and Lyndsey, workers at Kootenay Joe Farm, were standing in the field adjacent to the road, staring in his direction. Assuming it was all about him, Roger waved and smiled at them as he drove past.

At the junction of Kootenay Joe Road and Holmgren Road he stopped, looked left for traffic, then looked right. What he saw was puzzling. About a hundred metres up the road, past the trees that bordered Rachel's property, was a metres-deep wall of debris. Obviously he was looking at a landslide, but what was it doing there on the road, so far from the creek?

Richard Ortega and Gerry Rogers's first thought was for Christopher and me. They abandoned the smart meter installer, raced down Kootenay Joe Road in Richard's red truck and stopped beside Roger. "We're going down to Chris and Mandy's place. Want to come?" They were completely focused on what might have happened down the creek, and didn't once look up the road in the direction of Val Webber's house. Roger hesitated for a moment then joined them and they sped down the road, followed closely by neighbour Tony Holland on his ATV and Kyle, the smart meter installer, in his truck.

Patrick Steiner, Colleen O'Brien, and Patrick and Carol O'Brien

Across the road at Kootenay Joe Farm, the young owners, Patrick Steiner and Colleen O'Brien, were preparing to take their three-week-old son, Maël, to Kaslo for his routine hearing test. Colleen's parents, Patrick and Carol O'Brien, had arrived two days before in their camper van, from their home in Mission, BC, to meet their first grandchild. The grandparents were out in the yard fitting a roof rack onto the kids' car while Patrick was using a chainsaw nearby, wearing hearing protectors.

Patrick and Carol O'Brien could not see the landslide over the ridge, but heard what they realized later were the three stages of its passage. In the first few seconds it sounded like a train approaching, or sand in a funnel, getting rapidly louder. Colleen hurried outside with the baby because she could feel the house shaking. She signalled to her husband to take off his hearing protectors.

A huge explosion of sound, ten times greater than before, engulfed them. The ground shook and Patrick O'Brien said later it was like being bombarded by boulders. The din then ceased abruptly, and they heard what they presumed was the tail end of the slide ripping on down the creek with a whooshing, snapping noise. The family stood together, dumbfounded. O'Brien estimates the whole thing was over in about forty-five seconds.

Peter and Bobbi Huber

In Birchdale, a tiny, water-access-only community about five kilometres south of Johnson's Landing, Peter Huber was doing some maintenance on the dock, pounding spikes into wood. Peter and his wife, Bobbi, have lived in Birchdale since 1976. They love the remoteness, the commute by boat across the lake and the absence of infrastructure. Phones are of the radio or satellite type, and their solar and hydro power is generated locally.

Peter was absorbed in his work yet at the same time aware of everything happening around him across the broad expanse and stunning sweep of north Kootenay Lake. He heard a far-off rumbling and paused, wondering if it was dry lightning or an approaching thunderstorm, but the sky was clear and he resumed his work. A few seconds later came another rumble. This time he stopped, sat back on his heels and looked north over the water towards Kootenay Joe Ridge. He saw a cloud of airborne material, but couldn't see where it had originated because Gar Creek was behind the ridge and below his field of vision.

Peter dropped his tools and hurried up the trail to the house to tell Bobbi; she'd also heard something. A little while later their neighbours Robert Nellis and Sheila Murray-Nellis appeared at the door to say cups had been rattling on the table, and they were afraid something big had happened. They turned on the radio and within a very short time heard a breaking news story on CBC. Robert, a nurse at the Victorian Hospital of Kaslo, decided to go with Sheila over to Johnson's Landing by boat to see if anyone needed help.

Over in Johnson's Landing, Gerry, Richard, Roger, Bob, Harvey, Tony and Kyle crowded around Renata, who was shaking visibly, and still standing on the spot where she'd stopped running down the driveway. Muddy silt seeped across the lawn and through the garden. She told them, "Mandy's in Kaslo, Christopher's in Oregon, Kurt's in Toronto!" Somebody added: "Thank God! And you're here!"

Everyone cheered up with the knowledge that Christopher and I weren't in the house. But when Roger explained that the slide had also come across Holmgren Road—to Val's house—they leapt to their feet. They recall being in a sweat, pounding back up the meadow, manoeuvring to extract their vehicles from the parking jam at Creek Corner. Roger hopped on the back of Tony's ATV; those two were the first of the group to arrive at Val Webber's house.

Roger climbed onto the Webbers' roof, but Rachel Rozzoni, standing nearby with her children, yelled at him to be careful because power lines lay everywhere. From his vantage point he looked out over an otherworldly scene. A vast area was covered and completely devastated—it was not the little finger of wreckage he'd envisaged. Val's chimney was poking out of the mud not quite where it ought to be. Yet the untouched corner of the yard looked so peaceful with its green grass, fruit trees and barn—and there beside the barn stood two parked cars.

Bob Yetter remembers working on pure adrenalin as he pulled into Val's driveway. He scrambled onto the roof to join Roger. The gable was filled to the brim with mud, and beams were popping. Both men realized it was hopeless. Mud up to the rafters and the house displaced—no hollow or space where people might still be breathing. They hollered into the void but Bob, as he reported later, had already made up his mind that no reply would mean no one was alive.

Roger heard John Madill's air horn and went to investigate, leaving Bob on the roof. He followed an old trail below the toe of the slide, and found John, his face bloody, standing beside his house, signalling uphill towards Petra's. The two men attempted to clamber over to her place, but the forested hillside had become an open field of deep soft muck with nothing to stand on. There was no destination either. Petra's house had disappeared.

Roger was uncomfortably aware of the creek draw, denuded of its trees: he didn't like the sound or feel of it. He told John he thought they should get out of there, and they raced back around the toe of the slide, passing Harvey, now on his ATV.

Eager to inspect the damage to his pottery studio and anxious about what he would find, Harvey drove up his forest trail, cleared the ridge and met a spooky, surreal scene. The grass and buildings immediately in front of him looked normal; the slide flow had actually stopped at the studio's doorstep. But logs had shot forward like spears, with such velocity they'd run right through the buildings and knocked them crooked.

He explored around the Madills' house on foot. A timber was sticking out of the west wall and his immediate bizarre thought was, "John must be doing some work on the house." But when he walked round the corner, he saw that the wall had been hit from inside by a huge tree that had barrelled straight through the living room and kitchen.

At Petra's there wasn't anything left to see. Bewildered and disoriented, not knowing what else to do, Harvey took himself home and decided to finish the task he'd started that morning: making hay. He mowed hay like a robot, all afternoon, in the same traumatized, helpless way that I resumed my lawn mowing in Kaslo after learning that our house no longer existed. It seemed absolutely reasonable, in that moment of intense shock, to try to carry on as though nothing had happened.

HUSAR task force examines the Webbers' buried house.

Chapter 9: First Reactions

On that Thursday, in the space of barely a minute, a rapid debris avalanche, 320,000 cubic metres in volume, broke free from the mountain and descended the narrow Gar Creek channel at speeds approaching 150 kilometres per hour. According to the geotechnical findings published by the Regional District of the Central Kootenay in the *Johnson's Landing Landslide Hazard and Risk Assessment* in May of 2013, half the debris climbed out of the creek channel, crested a low ridge and spread out southwards across the bench, covering a six-and-a-half-hectare area. Less than 5 percent of the debris, comprised of mainly trees, travelled on down the creek channel to the lake. The remaining 45 percent of the debris completely filled the channel from bank to bank along much of its length for almost twenty-four hours.

The tiny community of Johnson's Landing was cut in half.

Inhabitants of the north side of Gar Creek still had the twisty, single-lane, unpaved road to the highway that led to Kaslo, but the south side was stranded, accessible only by water, by helicopter or by climbing over the mud and tree debris that filled the creek draw. On Thursday many people crossed back and forth over the slide, oblivious to the danger.

Richard Ortega and Gerry Rogers were the first ones who scaled the mud wall from the post office cabin side of our driveway, and climbed across the slide to our house. At least ten other neighbours scrambled down the north bank of the creek to look for Christopher and me. Roger's partner Carol was one of the first, followed by Richard Taylor, Susan Grimble, their daughter, Lila, and Richard's two granddaughters, aged ten and eleven. One close friend of ours, retired anaesthesiologist Roland Procter, ran down the hillside armed with a pick and shovel, thinking he might help to clear some "minor debris" off the driveway. Lew McMillan went with him. They were followed soon afterwards by Bill Wells and Greg Utzig, who'd driven to the Landing after reading Loran's alarming emails. They arrived just fifteen minutes after the landslide came down.

Everyone clambered onto the gently sloping deck. Richard Ortega later described how the house seemed to groan in its death agony as beams snapped and glass shattered deep inside, and the collapsed structure settled under the weight of rocks and trees. The spectacle was incongruous—bright red geraniums in pots still clung to the edge of the deck; the lake was lapping; sunshine dappled the vibrant green foliage and ripped branches that formed an almost impenetrable hedge around the house. Birdsong rose into the deep blue sky, and under it lay our house, folded up and flattened. A house that had been part of everyone's life: solid and certain; a piece of the past, a last link to Ruth Burt.

Roland called my name through a broken window. It was pitch-dark inside, he recalls, with the roof collapsed, but he saw a narrow space where the roof rested on the dining table. Everywhere lay rubble: furniture, fittings, chinaware, crushed and smashed. He remembers a cascade of books fanned out over a patch of floor and the fridge condensed to the size of a microwave oven.

Hearing no response, Roland hiked back up the hill, arriving at the road just as the ambulance from Kaslo pulled up. He told Amanda and Orion, the two paramedics, that he was afraid I might be trapped inside the house, and guided them down the bank with their resuscitation equipment, oxygen and first aid kits.

Lila, Susan, Richard and the grandkids negotiated their way gingerly between the muddy tree trunks and crossed the slide to the driveway. They cupped their mouths and shouted our names. They found Renata near the post office cabin talking to Jesse Howardson, who'd hurried down from Kootenay Joe Farm. "They're safe," Renata cried. "Mandy went to Kaslo and Christopher's in Oregon with Mom."

Jesse Howardson was a new arrival in the Landing. She didn't know Lila Taylor and, of course, didn't know about her close relationship with Diana. Had she known, she would have shared her dreadful news less bluntly. But she simply blurted out: "The Webbers' house is gone!" Everybody froze. Renata, still hugging Lila, turned to look at Jesse: "What about Val and the girls? Where are they?"

Lila looked at Jesse, confused and perplexed—her words didn't make sense. Lila had spoken to Diana on the phone just before breakfast, not half an hour ago. What in the world was Jesse talking about?

Lila remembers a sudden surge of anguish coursing through her body. She broke free from Renata and ran pell-mell, blonde hair flying, up the steep trail through the woods to the community hall. Blinded by sweat pouring into her eyes, panting and soaked, she bumped into Rachel Rozzoni, who'd driven her children to the community hall for safety. "What's happened to the Webbers' house?" Rachel wouldn't meet her eye and was reluctant to say anything. What was going on? Lila grabbed hold of Rachel. "Diana phoned me just a few minutes ago. She's in the house! You've got to take me up there!"

Rachel couldn't allow Lila to witness that dreadful scene alone. All the mud, only the roof visible. Lila looked distraught; who knew what she might do? Rachel turned to the children. "Aidan. Giselle. Stay inside the hall. Look after your baby sister. Read her a story. I'll be back just as soon as I can."

They climbed into Rachel's green Jetta. She parked outside the Webbers' fence. Diana's bronze RAV and Val's silver Subaru were standing in exactly the right place, the place they always parked. The front corner of the yard was almost normal. By now, however, Lila knew from Rachel's face that something terrible had happened. Both women were shaking as they tiptoed over the sunlit, manicured lawn, which stopped abruptly at a three-metre-high wall of beige mud that stank and oozed slowly forward. Close to hysteria, they giggled nervously. "Val would be so mad to see his cherished yard in such a mess," Rachel whispered.

Lila gazed around, open-mouthed. Only the ripped-away roof and gables were visible. The soft, rubble-filled mud, like liquid cement, made glooping, gurgling noises as it settled, and had infiltrated every cranny. The stink was terrible. Lila pinched her nose between her fingers. Diana! She remembered their last excursion in the boat on Tuesday. They'd been imagining, lightheartedly, in what manner they might die, and Diana said, "Margie had a dream that my house was buried under mud."

Just forty-eight hours later Margie's apocalyptic vision had been fulfilled. Lila took a step forward and sank up to her knee.

The two women looked at one another and then at the disaster, struck dumb by an overwhelming emptiness. They didn't sob or utter a single word. After a few minutes of standing in the baking heat, sweat trickling down their backs, they climbed into Rachel's car and sat there quietly, their heads lowered. Lila felt sick to her stomach. Rachel turned the key in the ignition and drove the Jetta slowly back down the road to the community hall.

THE PHONES STILL worked in most of the undamaged houses on the south side. Difficult calls had to be made. Renata phoned Paul Hunter in Kaslo and could tell by his voice that he didn't know. "You haven't heard what happened?"

Paul replied, "Oh yes, I heard you and Mandy saved the day yesterday and diverted the creek!"

Renata took a deep breath to fight back tears. "Oh no, Paul, that's not it. Something much bigger has happened. Their home is gone. And there's worse…"

After phoning me, Renata talked to Virginia in Oregon. "Mom, you've got to tell Christopher that he still has a wife and a sister—but no home anymore." She also phoned her daughter Margie, in Vancouver, who answered the call walking up to the front door of the house where she worked as a nanny. She slumped down on the steps, incapacitated by the news and by a jolt of recognition: in her dream six weeks earlier she'd "known" the Webbers all lay dead under the landslide.

Lila recognized that she was the one who had to phone Lynn Migdal. "Oh, why don't you wait until the sniffer dogs can go in and check the house," someone said, but Lila shook her head. She'd seen the house. She composed herself and placed the call to Florida. "Lynn? It's Lila."

How do you explain to a mother that her two daughters, her ex-husband and their home have just been wiped out? Lila heard Lynn inhale sharply, as if she knew from Lila's first words that something was terribly wrong. Lila took a breath herself and said simply, "There was a landslide. It's hard to believe, I know. Everyone's buried. People are coming to search but it doesn't look hopeful."

Lila knew it would be impossible for Lynn to grasp the scale of this monstrous thing, like a hound of hell, that had devoured her family and swallowed the house. People could not comprehend its immensity, its non-negotiable brute power as it slammed into the side of one house, missed another, buried a third—unless they saw it for themselves.

ERIC SCHINDLER AND his wife, Sailan, knew nothing about the disaster. Their airy log house stands about 750 metres away from the slide's path, around a headland, north of Gar Creek. Eric is a retired nature photographer from Germany, with an abiding, lifelong passion for the wildlife of the Kootenays. Sailan was born and raised in Hong Kong, and had a career as an interior designer in Ontario. They've lived in Johnson's Landing for more than a quarter century. Longtime friends of the Rogers–Godbe household, they were also very close to Petra Frehse.

Their power went out at 10:37, and half an hour later they heard the ambulance siren across the lake on the highway. Thirty minutes after that the siren was directly below them, coming up the hill. Their first thought was for their friend Linda Godbe, who required regular kidney dialysis at home. No one answered when they phoned her, and there was no reply at Petra's either, so they called the Johnson's Landing Retreat Centre, where the owner, Richard Ortega, assured Eric that everyone was okay. "Yes, but why *wouldn't* you be okay?" Eric asked in surprise. "Well... we've had a landslide. Here's Gerry." And Eric learned about the slide from Gerry Rogers, who was stranded on the south side with no easy way of getting back to his home, high on the north bank.

Eric and Sailan set out at once to check on Linda and Loran, taking an old back trail that climbed the hill through the woods towards Gar Creek. Eric, walking ahead of Sailan, caught the first glimpse of the wide beige gulley and screamed out: "No! No! No!" as he took in the mangled trees along the bank. The slide had leapt over the low hill to the north of Petra's cabin. That hill, studded with boulders and tree trunks, was now fifteen metres higher than it should be.

Up at the house they found Linda and Loran, pale and shaken but physically unharmed. The house had no power, water or phone, and no driveway access to the road. "We'll have to evacuate," Loran told them. "Linda can't do her kidney dialysis here."

Eric spied a Swainson's thrush on the ground. Usually an unobtrusive bird, it was behaving oddly. It hopped around in circles calling repeatedly; to Eric's naturalist's eye it looked distraught and bewildered, perhaps searching for its young— but all the trees were gone. As he would later say, "That little bird, for me, symbolized the horror and loss all four of us felt." They gazed helplessly up and down the gaping scar that split the landscape. The creek was not running properly, Eric noticed—the water was accumulating in pools. As he and Sailan headed down the trail he wondered what that would mean.

Back home, Eric contacted their friend Fred Rudolph in Kaslo because Fred had an internet connection. Eric needed a phone number for Petra's half-brother, Hans-Hubertus Vogt, in Germany. Petra had once given Eric a birthday gift of a mug that displayed the name of the town where her family lived. Using this information, Fred got on the computer and before long was able to give Eric the phone number.

Eric called Hans-Hubertus and asked him to break the news as gently as possible to Petra's mother. Ruth Vogt phoned Eric back almost immediately and told him about her phone call to Petra that morning. Ruth knew the exact time of their conversation, and it was devastating confirmation that Petra had indeed been at home, just moments before the slide came down. Eric's heart sank. Sailan buried her face in her hands.

THE PHONE AT Kootenay Joe Farm was in great demand. Patrick and Carol O'Brien policed the line so that local people could make outgoing calls between calls from journalists, who began phoning almost immediately. The farm was a gathering point for south-side residents. People were hungry, so Carol and Colleen cooked up a vat of pasta and fed everyone.

John Madill reached for the phone when his turn came and called Jillian at her mother's house in Kaslo. Jillian later recalled his acute agitation and exact words: "You'd better come back. Our house is gone. Petra's dead. Val and the girls are dead. There's no sign of them." Too stunned to take it all in, Jillian didn't think to ask John how he was doing, but told him, "That's enough for now. Look after yourself. I'll be back as soon as I can." She apparently said a few other things too, because John remarked afterwards to Patrick O'Brien, "I've been married to Jillian for forty-six years and I never heard her use *those* cuss words before!"

Rachel drove the children to Kootenay Joe Farm to phone Dan Tarini, Aidan and Giselle's father. Aidan punched in the numbers and spoke to him first, struggling to make his dad understand what had happened. Dan was in Kaslo, standing with his friend Deane in Deane's yard, enjoying the sunny morning. Dan laughed—he thought his son was playing a joke on him.

Rachel grabbed the phone. "No, Dan, listen! There could be another slide. You've got to bring a boat. I have to get out with the kids!" In Kaslo, Deane watched as Dan's laughter died and his face blanched. This was no joke. Rachel was serious. "A massive landslide in Johnson's Landing," Dan told Deane. "I've got to get over there." Deane had a boat in the Kaslo marina and said simply, "Right. Let's get going." It took two boat trips to evacuate the family, their three chocolate Labrador dogs and a few necessities Dan quickly collected from the house.

MEANWHILE, ON THE north side of Gar Creek, Gail Spitler and Lynne Cannon's place on Rogers Road was also a communications hub. Their phone rang incessantly; they couldn't even sit down to grab a bite to eat, and were running high on adrenalin. Deb Borsos, the local emergency contact person for wildfires and other events, called them from her home in Argenta, wanting a list of who was missing. Overhead, helicopters circled, filming the ravaged landscape. Reporters were among the first responders to the disaster. The helicopters landed in the field beside Rogers Road with a deafening din, the wind from their blades flattening the grass and raising clouds of dust.

The silver Buick drove slowly up Rogers Road at around one thirty. Jillian was desperately anxious to see John and the subsequent wait seemed endless. Lynne welcomed her indoors. "You're going to stay here overnight. You can use the trailer. Stay as long as you need to."

After phoning Jillian from Kootenay Joe Farm, John made his way down to the beach. Robert and Sheila Nellis from Birchdale found him there, looking lost and dazed, and ferried him around the slide in their boat. John trudged up Rogers Road at around four p.m., worn out, grey with dust, his face bloodstained and ashen.

Linda Portman and Mary Linn of BC's Emergency Social Services (ESS) program were sent to Johnson's Landing that afternoon to assist the evacuees. They arrived by water and had to climb a steep hillside trail to reach the community hall. The hall was hot and uncomfortable, with no power or phone, and nothing to eat. The O'Brien–Steiner family received their vouchers for food, clothing and a first night's accommodation at the Kaslo Motel, but then spent long hours waiting to evacuate, sustained by nothing more than a couple of granola bars.

On Harvey's ATV, RCMP corporal Chris Backus conveyed messages between ESS and Search and Rescue (SAR) until, eventually, Patrick O'Brien came up with the solution: why not let them travel to Kaslo on the Nelson SAR boat, which needed to return to base before nightfall? The SAR boat dropped the family at the Kaslo marina around nine p.m. but left them there on the dock, stranded, with their tiny baby, the dog and copious baggage. Carol ran round the bay to persuade the pizza restaurant not to close just yet. Patrick Steiner flagged down two passersby who brought vehicles and transported the exhausted family and their luggage to the motel.

Lew McMillan lost track of Roland after searching at our place, and made his way home to his wife, Susan Archibald. On Rogers Road police cars were parked everywhere. RCMP sergeant Tim MacDonald introduced himself and asked Lew where he lived, and whether he knew the local area. When Lew affirmed that he did, MacDonald deputized him as a community resource person on the scene. Lew spent a busy afternoon providing information to the emergency responders, including a map that showed the property lines. He handed out the community's walkie-talkies, and used his vehicle to transport officials up and down the road. The atmosphere was chaotic and no one seemed to know what was going on.

At the end of Thursday the bottom of Rogers Road, below Gail and Lynne's property, was a parking hub for eight police cars, two SAR trucks, various Regional District of Central Kootenay (RDCK) officials' cars, the ambulance and the first responders' vehicles. At least a dozen RCMP officers, including two dog handlers, and SAR volunteers from Kaslo and Nelson milled around in some frustration. Everyone was under strict orders not to cross the creek because of the danger. On the periphery stood Lew, in a faded cap, shorts and a shirt caked in mud from climbing over the slide.

The emergency personnel mustered in a huddle and Lew heard them say, "That's all we can do today. Tomorrow we concentrate on searching for four people at the Webber home." Lew sighed in exasperation. He, Lila and Sailan had repeatedly refuted the official line that all four missing persons were in the same house. Everyone in the community knew Petra could not possibly have been having breakfast at the Webbers' house when the girls were there: Val and Petra had a relationship, and Val's daughters didn't approve. And anyway, it was already known now that Petra had been on the phone to her mother at her own home just before the slide.

Lew stepped up and interjected politely, "We don't think that's true." The spokesperson spun round and confronted him: "And who the hell are you? I don't think we've been introduced." Lew, abashed, stepped back. He'd spent the whole day in the hot sun, assisting as a community representative. But these outsiders apparently had no interest in his local knowledge and expertise. Why, he wondered, did they have to be so abrupt?

The phone at Richard Taylor's house rang and rang. Each time Lila picked it up she was apprehensive—news people asking questions. Misinformation ran rampant: "Don't worry, the girls are in town." "They've been seen in Nelson." "They're in the basement!" But the house didn't have a basement, just a narrow crawl space and a root cellar. And even if there *had* been a basement, the mud slurry would have filled every void. People were imagining earthquake scenarios. This was nothing like an earthquake.

Someone even called Lynn Migdal in Florida and told her the girls were safe and well in Nelson. Margie contacted her mother, Renata, after a posting on Facebook announced that the Webbers had been found alive. Lila and Renata, who'd moved to the Taylors' house for safety, had to keep saying: "No! It's not true! They're not fine! They're in their house."

It was awful, Lila was to realize later, to have to argue with people who wanted them to be alive, to have to be the bearer of bad news. No one wanted them alive more than Lila herself. But she'd been to the site of the house; she'd seen with her own eyes that her dearest friend Diana and her feisty younger sister, Rachel, could not have survived under that deep, dense mud. Nor Val, warm and open, a wonderful dad, who had always been so generous and fun to be around.

THAT EVENING, RENATA could not settle down. Lennie eyed his "mum" dolefully and plodded alongside, hot, tired and stiff. She took photographs of our collapsed house, wandered around bewildered, and watched as more and more water seeped out of the mud, first on one side of the slide, then on the other. She returned to the Taylors' house.

Ren had not yet seen the Webbers' house for herself and still imagined that Val and the girls were buried but somehow alive and in need of urgent help. As darkness fell, she set off once more from the Taylors' house, compelled to find out, evading the last RCMP officer still on duty patrolling the road. She ran down the trail, leapt into the canoe and launched onto the lake. She paddled along the shoreline past the slide. The helicopters had stopped for the night and the silent darkness enshrouded her like a mantle. Bats out hunting swooped and fluttered over the starlit water. It would have been so easy to let the canoe drift and allow the gentle swell to lull her into blissful forgetfulness. She yearned to escape this nightmare but there was no escape.

Renata dragged the canoe on shore and forced her aching limbs to carry her up the hill one more time, past the community hall and onwards to the Fry Creek trailhead. The road unwound in the gloom, looking so familiar she thought, *Maybe it isn't true; perhaps everyone's mistaken and nothing bad has happened.*

In front of her rose the wall of debris, solidified, looking like a mass that belonged in outer space. A moonscape.

She scaled a sloping tree trunk and stood on the Webbers' roof, like so many others had done that day. Peering uphill through the semi-darkness of a midsummer's night she finally understood what everyone was trying to tell her. This thing was gigantic! Nobody could help Val and the girls now. She inhaled the night air deeply into her lungs. It held no refreshment; it was stagnant and foul, like a bog. Too exhausted even to cry out, gritting her teeth, concentrating on every step, she stumbled back to the beach and made her way around the slide, back to the Taylors' house.

Renata and Lila slept together on the porch bed that night, with loyal old Lennie slumped on the floor beside them. Ren had spoken to me in Kaslo at around eight p.m. and knew about my plan to come next morning with Osa in Deane's boat, in search of Ozzie. She advised me to land the boat on the north side of the house for easier access to the deck.

IN THE EARLY hours of Friday morning, Roland Procter awoke to a noise behind his house and saw headlights whip past his woodshed. He jumped out of bed, dressed quickly and drove down to Rogers Road where he found an RCMP officer asleep in his vehicle. Roland woke him. The officer claimed he'd seen nothing (and denied he'd been asleep).

Back home, Roland couldn't let the image go. He'd seen headlights. He climbed on his ATV and followed the old back road that Eric and Sailan had hiked on Thursday, up-hill to the north bank of Gar Creek where the trail was cut off by the landslide. There he found Robin Hoy, a resident of Argenta, standing on the bank in the half-light of dawn, filming and taking photographs. Robin, despite an artificial leg, was preparing to hike down into the slide path. He seemed very excited by events. Roland talked to Robin for a while then returned home to bed.

Over the next few hours Robin crossed the creek, toured the landslide area and filmed the abandoned buildings inside and out. He posted his video on YouTube.

LILA AWOKE WITH a start that morning, and the memories of the day before flooded back. Her eyes filled with tears. She slipped quietly out of bed in order not to disturb Ren, stepped carefully over the snoring bulk of Lennie, pulled on her clothes and ran up the road to the newly established command post on Rogers Road to see if there was any news of Diana.

In her sensitized state Lila was acutely aware of how the police treated her requests for information. The non-local police struck her as both rude and dismissive. "They told me they could not divulge information to the public. I am not the public! Their attitude seemed to be, we're dealing with this. You're in the way. Go away!"

She found the Kaslo RCMP and local SAR much kinder and more understanding of her need to ask about Diana. "Sergeant Tim Little put his hand on my shoulder, took me aside, told me everything he knew, and invited me to sit there and hang out. He said he'd tell me immediately if there was any news. His helpfulness calmed me down."

Lew McMillan found Lila sitting by the command post, wringing her hands, with tears pouring down her cheeks. Together they tried again to tell the RCMP that Petra had been in her own home on Thursday morning. But the official story didn't change until late on Saturday—more than twenty-four hours later—when the RCMP finally announced that an active search for Petra was now underway at the site of her own house.

Lila was nonplussed and upset by the reporters who confronted her at every turn, pointing microphones and assailing her with a barrage of questions. She took refuge for the next several hours at Lew and Susan's home, having tea and staying out of the media spotlight.

JUST AFTER TEN o'clock on Friday, July 13, Renata heard the thunderous roar of the second landslide. She gazed out of the Taylors' kitchen window in disbelief as the entire contents of the creek channel turned into waves of liquid mud that flushed the remaining rock and tree debris down the ravine. Renata begged Richard and Susan to evacuate with the grandchildren, and was horrified when Richard demurred.

With frenzied gesticulation and tears, she tried to make them understand the danger they were in, as she perceived it, and the need to evacuate the grandchildren to a place of safety. Great pulses of mud poured down the creek below the

Taylors' house, booming and crashing, ripping out trees. She finally persuaded Richard and Susan and they grabbed some things and drove away with the grandkids. The second slide continued to disgorge the creek contents into the lake for more than an hour.

Renata wondered where Lila had gone, but was even more anxious about me, knowing my plan to return to our house by water. She said later, "I thought I'd led you to your death, telling you to land on the north shore. You'd said what time you'd be coming. I knew you must be down there!" Ren also wondered about her car, and her belongings in the post office cabin. Had they been swept away by the morning's mudslide?

She left the Taylors' house. At the rescue command post on Rogers Road they denied any knowledge of Lila, even though she'd been there several times asking for news.

Renata had reached the end of her strength. "I was trying to run, but my body wouldn't respond." She stumbled up Rogers Road to Gail and Lynne's house and they helped her indoors. Ren remembers, "I was in complete agony, thinking you were dead, and maybe Lila too. But I couldn't go back down the hill again to find out. I hadn't bathed or eaten. I was completely exhausted."

Lynne had watched Renata approaching up the driveway. "Her face was grotesquely taut, frozen in a mask of anguish. She was breathless, in a terrible panic for Lila's and your safety. Indoors, she stood in a corner of our living room whispering over and over: 'I don't know what to do.' I told her, 'You're not going to do anything. You can't right now. Just stay here.' Gradually she calmed down. I told her to eat anything she felt like. I found her some fresh clothes, she had a bath and washed her hair, I gave her a dressing gown, and she sat outside in the sunshine."

Renata had no words to express her gratitude until later. "Lynne took care of us all. She had John and Jillian in housecoats! She'd fed them and they'd slept there overnight." The ugly scar across the hillside was invisible from their house, and their garden was an island of beauty filled with flowers and shrubs, birdfeeders and shady trees. A refuge where, temporarily, they could lay down their burdens and rest.

GAIL AND LYNNE offered assistance of many kinds on Thursday and Friday. Bob Keating of CBC Radio filed his first reports from their telephone because there's no cellphone coverage in the Landing. Reporters knocked on the door for interviews. There were no toilets for the emergency response people in the first two days, so people used Gail and Lynne's bathroom. The tenant on the farm bordering Rogers Road abruptly forbade any more helicopter landings in his field, claiming he was going to make hay. Lynne helped identify alternative places to land, and they marked out a new helipad west of Lew and Susan's driveway.

Gail and Lynne's house was packed on Friday. Besides John, Jillian and Renata, two emergency response women spent time on the phone arranging for Jillian's replacement medications to be sent from the pharmacy in Kaslo. The Emergency Social Services (ESS) representatives, Linda Portman and Maggie Crowe, arrived in the afternoon and Gail explained to Renata that she could get assistance from them. "But I'm not a victim!" Ren kept saying. Gail and Lynne worked hard to convince her that she was indeed eligible for help. In Ren's mind, victims were people who lived in the Landing and had lost houses and possessions.

ESS gave Renata vouchers for food, clothing and a night's accommodation at the Hume Hotel in Nelson. Renata would have to drive to Castlegar early on Saturday to pick up Margie from the airport. That Friday afternoon the ESS transported Ren to Kaslo, halfway to Nelson. In Kaslo Ren borrowed a friend's car and drove to Nelson. The staff of the Hume Hotel received her with warmth and exceptional consideration. On Saturday morning she picked up Lila at her family's house in Nelson and they continued down the road another half-hour to Castlegar airport to meet Margie's early flight from Vancouver.

JOHNSON'S LANDING, IN the days following the landslides, was a ghost town. Out of a population of around forty before the slides, nine residents remained on the south side, and fourteen on the north side. Megan Cole, a journalist with the *Nelson Star*, recalled the desolate scene that greeted her when she visited by boat on Sunday, July 15. "We walked up to houses on the south side looking for those who had chosen to stay behind. We knocked on doors and looked in windows. It was eerie and quiet. Houses abandoned with coffee cups and breakfast left on the table because everyone left in a hurry."

Bob Yetter had opted not to evacuate, and made himself useful around the south side. He ran people's generators to keep fridges and freezers going until power was restored, fed and watered goats and chickens at Kootenay Joe Farm—everyone had evacuated by this time—and helped pump water from the lake into a holding tank on a truck, delivering it to households in need.

On Sunday, Derek Baker needed another hand as crew on his barge, which he was using to ship stranded vehicles across the lake, so Bob made a trip across to Schroeder Creek and back. He was also hired by the RDCK to work as a security officer, controlling access into the Landing by road and ensuring vacant property remained safe. He didn't leave Johnson's Landing for twelve days. Like so many people living in isolated rural households, Bob had resources, including plenty of food on hand: canned and frozen goods, plus abundant fresh produce from the vegetable garden.

Residents might have been thin on the ground, but the slide area throbbed with activity. Over a hundred responders poured in from across the province to assist the rescue effort.

Vancouver's Heavy Urban Search and Rescue (HUSAR) task force dispatched fifty-five personnel and two truckloads of equipment, arriving in Kaslo on Friday afternoon.

On Saturday, Bob Yetter observed with interest as the HUSAR task force set to work in the slide area, appreciative of their good intentions, bravery and commitment. "They gave their hearts and sweat to what must be an incredibly difficult and often thankless job."

However, the task force members did not know the lay of the land or the exact location of the Webber and Frehse house sites. Landing residents, on the other hand, knew their local geography intimately. Bob Yetter went to the command post, ready to assist. "I expected that, once they were set up, they'd call the locals together and get information from us."

But the meeting Bob was expecting didn't happen. HUSAR didn't request or appear to want local information and Bob was surprised by their standoffishness. "We were basically treated like we were in the way. As if by choosing to stay and look after our community's interests instead of evacuating, we were some kind of rogue semi-criminal element." Whenever Bob approached the command post he was greeted by, "What do you need, Bob?" and given his cue to leave.

When Bob saw that they were digging in a spot far away from the Webbers' house, he confronted them. "I approached the command post to ask them—since they had neglected to ask us, and it had become clear that there was to be no formal interaction with the community members—if they wanted to know the location of the Webber house, since they were digging in the wrong place.

"I told them I'd worked on the Webbers' house, did maintenance for Val, and had even stayed there for a few weeks, so could easily show them the correct location. I was 'put on hold' for some two hours and left standing around in the heat until the guy in charge had time to talk to me.

"While I waited I drew a diagram of the house orientation and layout, and its relation to still existing landmarks. An RCMP police dog handler concurred with the spot I identified and said, 'That's what my dog's telling me, too, but they're not listening to me either!'" Bob eventually got a chance to explain his diagram to the person in command. He was invited onto the site to help mark the corners of the house, and they started digging a fresh hole.

Three months later, Bob wrote a letter to Gundula Brigl, the regional manager for the southern interior at Emergency Management BC.

Hours and even days were lost in this case due to poor intelligence as to the location to be searched. All they had to do was ask. Local knowledge is perhaps not worth much in an urban area—I don't know—but in a rural area like this, people often know their neighbors' property, habits, and behavior.

All those guys needed was one person—one of those hundred or so people who were on-site here—to go and interact with the people of this community. Someone whose job it was to meet with community members, tell them what they were doing, and to try and glean any useful information.

Sure, that person will have to deal with excited stories, emotional concerns, useless nonsense, and even hysteria from a traumatized people, but the right person could both calm the situation AND sift out the information or individuals useful to their search efforts.

Chapter 10: Those Who Came

I WANT TO pause for a moment, step back from the fray and consider how people respond to trauma. In my years of working in hospice, I'd learned that a first reaction to trauma is disbelief and denial. Anyone who has ever experienced a devastating surprise will recognize how slow the mind is to accept what has happened. How you can stand and look at a four-metre-high stretch of rubble, as people in Johnson's Landing did, and work out a reason why it would be there, a reason that did *not* include half the mountain having slid into the creek, hauling tons of debris, then jumping a bank and burying houses that weren't nearby.

The brain responds to the event by refusing to take it in. It's as though the brain says, "No, I'm sorry, this can't be true. It doesn't fit into what I know and understand. I can't allow it." Anyone who loses a husband, wife, partner or child due to a fatal accident or sudden death, anyone receiving a terrible diagnosis, anyone caught in a tsunami, or an earthquake or a landslide—the first reaction is disbelief.

People in shock return to the scene of devastation over and over again, just to look, because it's hard to believe their eyes. Denial seems also to be an initial reaction (a reaction that can settle in for some people). As a result of these two responses to disaster, most of us try to carry on as though nothing has happened. In Johnson's Landing, people climbed into cars and drove down the road even though they *knew* it was washed out. Someone observed a displaced log in a wall and wondered if the owner was doing work on the house.

Slowly it comes to us: our world has shifted. As days pass we begin to realize that the comforting daily customs with family and friends are over. The safe and predictable routines are over. In time, some of us stumble mentally, trip and fall. For everyone, stress hormones kick in. Adrenalin causes physical symptoms: a thumping heart, nausea, headaches, abdominal pains, breathing difficulties. For me, amnesia took me by surprise. Afterwards people reminded me about conversations we'd had during that first afternoon. Andy Shadrack and Kate O'Keefe both urged me not to go back by boat to look for Ozzie, but I have no recollection of any such conversations.

Over subsequent days I noticed, in myself and others, a heightened anxiety and irritability. Sleeping was difficult and plagued by dreams and flashbacks. Our neighbours in the Landing reported feeling emotionally numb and detached from one another, wandering round their gardens in a mental fog, distracted, unable to concentrate or settle down. Normal tasks that yesterday seemed vital had today become meaningless.

You can imagine how the remaining denizens of Johnson's Landing felt when the first responders arrived, their adrenalin pumping for their own reasons. The first contingent arrived on Thursday afternoon in an explosion of noise and commotion. Vehicles roaring. Helicopters pounding overhead. Radios crackling. Shouts back and forth. On Friday afternoon, the HUSAR task force joined in. By Saturday the responders numbered over a hundred. Uniformed men (most of the HUSAR task force members are men), trained with military precision and dedicated to helping others and saving lives, are suddenly everywhere, in a remote area that people chose for its quiet, independent lifestyle.

Worlds collided.

Emergency response is military in character, with a recognized chain of command, clear instructions and each individual performing strictly assigned tasks. The responders, focused on their roles, seem brusque, even aggressive. Civilians are typically ignored or treated dismissively, as impediments to the rescue protocol.

In my experience of the trauma of others, and now in my own experience, I realize that people still standing are fragile and sensitized. Intellectually they know that the responders have come to help. But it can be another appalling shock. Gripped by our own trauma, right after the slide, we didn't think about *them*. And we didn't realize that the responders, too, might be disorientated, frightened and soon exhausted, spurred forward by the imperative to find somebody alive under the debris.

These men and women, many of them city dwellers, were abruptly ripped out of their comfort zone of work and family life; and they, in turn, were oblivious to the rural people they encountered, whose quiet wilderness peace had been shattered, first by the landslides and then by their arrival. Residents were tormented by the hubbub—there was nowhere they could hide from the din of incessant helicopter traffic stuttering overhead. Dust filled the air; cars and trucks roared up and down the hill; sirens shrieked. Uniformed responders and police officers shouted instructions to one another; reporters pestered locals with cameras and microphones. The fields lay mashed and trampled by the well-intentioned invasion. These details might seem insignificant, but to the individuals suffering sudden loss, it was huge.

IN THE MONTHS following the landslides, I wanted to know more about what had gone on in the Landing while I was in Kaslo, adrift. By interviewing some of the people who came to help, I gained a new perspective on how events unfolded after the mountain gave way. Here are the stories of five people who stepped up during those traumatic days and first weeks.

- Corporal Chris Backus of the RCMP landed on the south side of Gar Creek within two hours of the first slide, and stayed in the Landing for a week.
- Bruce Walker, manager of Kaslo Search and Rescue, was the incident commander who coordinated the rescue mission and assisted Vancouver's Heavy Urban Search and Rescue (HUSAR) task force.
- Bob Stair, retired coroner and world-renowned forensic anthropology specialist, conducted the recovery operation on behalf of the BC Coroners Service.
- Deb Borsos, North Kootenay Lake's emergency contact person, became the RDCK's recovery manager for the Johnson's Landing disaster—a post she would hold for two years.
- Excavator operator Duncan Lake undertook essential and perilous digging projects beside and within the Gar Creek channel, assisting the community in a multitude of ways.

RCMP Corporal Chris Backus

While I was conducting interviews for this book, people repeatedly told me about a tall, dark-haired, good-looking young RCMP officer by the name of Chris Backus. Lila said, "He was a wonderful person. Chris Backus is the only police officer I know who hugged people!" Bob Yetter said, "Chris was *the* guy to be here. He knew how to fit in and be a human being while doing his job as RCMP. He wasn't an ass. He wasn't authoritarian. He went way above and beyond the call of duty." Bob's neighbour Roger agreed: "Chris Backus was great. He did his job really well, and was diligent and unobtrusive."

A year after the landslides I found Chris at his current

posting in the Comox Valley on Vancouver Island. During his thirteen-year career with the RCMP all his postings have been in BC, apart from a period spent in Ivory Coast, West Africa, serving as a police officer for the United Nations. Returning from that troubled, war-torn country in 2009, Chris moved to the sleepy village of Kaslo. In July 2012, he was thirty-six years old and had just two months remaining in Kaslo.

Chris flew over the landslide around noon on Thursday, and had the helicopter drop him on the south side, where he set to work assessing the scene, confirming who was missing and arranging evacuations. He stayed. After his radio batteries went down, the locals wondered if the RCMP had forgotten about him. Bob Yetter recalled with a smile, "They didn't come back and get him and he didn't have anything! He just stayed here and we took care of him, fed him, gave him a place to sleep, a change of clothes and a toothbrush."

Chris talked frankly and thoughtfully with me about that week in July. Here is his story, mostly in his own words.

"Kaslo was by far the best posting of my career because of the sense of community. I'd never experienced a place like this before. You had the 'dirty dozen' as in any town, but the values of the community as a whole were above average.

"If I walked down Front Street in uniform it could take an hour. There were hugs! It was joyous! Even the high school kids—who in other places like to badmouth the cops—gave me hugs. Kaslo took me by storm and I still miss it very much.

"As a police officer, I think you need to belong to a community, and only then look at it from a policing perspective. We in the RCMP are transient—we know our start and end date, then we move on. I try not to be 'just' a law-enforcement officer. My first priority is to make the place my home, my community, and be a good community member. You have to show people you're a human being. As a culture, the RCMP sometimes forgets its humanity: when cops hang out only with cops they tend to see the world through a black and white lens.

"I knew Kaslo would have the black and the white, but also the wonderful multitude of greys in between, and I wanted to know them all. Once the community realized that, people trusted me, came to me, were honest, and I could do my job in a community-minded way. I received some criticism about getting too close to the community but I have no regrets. No doubt I made mistakes, but I wouldn't change much of what I did. On leaving Kaslo I felt I'd had a human experience rather than just a professional one.

"On the morning of July 12, 2012, I was in the police station. Tim MacDonald—a new officer, just arrived in Kaslo and still learning about his community—would often come in and say, 'Chris, we've got a situation here,' and would go on to describe people I knew well and had been dealing with for three years.

"Tim came in and said, 'Chris, I think we've got a situation here.' I laughed and said, 'Come on into my office, Tim, and we'll talk about it. And I'm probably going to guarantee you that it's *not* a situation!' Tim continued, 'We're getting reports of a landslide in Johnson's Landing, that several houses are buried and people are unaccounted for.'

"I leaped out of my chair. '*What*? I'm sorry, Tim, but this time you're right! This is a *major* f-----g situation!' I jumped in the truck and started up the road with lights and sirens blazing. I got onto the dispatch: 'Okay, you need to tell PEP [the Provincial Emergency Program]. We have to assume this is serious.'

"I arrived about an hour later to find the road washed out. I couldn't see what had happened so I began crawling down the bank towards the creek. Brian McMillan from YRB [Yellowhead Road Bridge, the highways maintenance contractor for the area] yelled at me, 'Get back up here right now! It's much too dangerous!' What stays in my mind to this day is the smell of earth. I never smelt earth of that intensity before. It stank.

"Someone landed a helicopter on our [north] side. I grabbed Bud Carlson and we jumped in. I told the pilot, 'We need to go up, look around and then I need you to drop me on the other side.' I knew Bud had grown up in Johnson's Landing and he'd be an excellent resource to give us the scenario. We flew over the scene and I asked Bud what he could tell me. There was silence. After a minute he said, 'Holy shit. This is something else.' Then he recovered and pointed out which houses were missing. We flew over the slide several times; I could see people down below waving at me.

"The helicopter dropped me on the stranded side and I met Bob Yetter, Roger, Jesse and Megan. Bob should get a medal! As soon as I landed he gave me a list and said, 'That's who's missing.' He had it all figured out. This information told me where to focus our efforts.

"PEP was saying 'Wait, we're coming,' but I said to Bob, 'Let's see if we can hear anything.' He took me to the Webbers' place but I quickly realized this wasn't a house, just a roof. I estimated the height of mud against nearby houses, power poles and the treeline and I understood the depth and the density of it, with trees and rocks sticking out. You couldn't appreciate the massive destructiveness of the thing unless you were out there walking on it. It was tragic. My intuitive sense was: it's not good. Chances of survival are very low.

"I was getting information that there might be a pocket, and that voices had been heard, but that was nonsense. The media tried to play into the rumours to sensationalize the story. I felt it was amoral and unfair to the community. It gave people a false sense of hope. We needed to be accurate; high school kids in Kaslo were glued to the news broadcasts, clinging to any glimmer of hope.

"First we accounted for everyone, and confirmed who was missing. Then it was a matter of figuring if Linda Godbe or anyone else needed emergency care. Once we got that straight, then the frustration hit. Hurry up and wait. Don't do anything. Don't go on the slide. Cease and desist. You felt the community frustration; we only had a short window of opportunity. But to what extent do you risk human life to try to save it?"

One of the first things Chris Backus did was borrow Harvey Armstrong's ATV so he could move around quickly and arrange the evacuation of south-side residents. Bob Yetter opted to stay, along with about eight others. Chris and Bob worked late into the evening helping a number of families and individuals.

Chris's account of the second slide and what followed also shows his dedication to the people living in the Landing. "On Friday morning I was in Bob Yetter's house, on the phone to my RCMP dispatch in Kelowna, when I heard the second slide roar down behind me like a jet plane. Not more than twenty-five metres beyond Bob's window I saw trees swept away, some still standing vertical. I left the phone hanging by its cord, and the front door wide open, and ran for my life, jumped on the ATV and got out of there. I was terrified! I'd had no idea there'd be a second slide.

"There were all manner of provincial systemic processes I had to comply with, informing residents about evacuation and landslide risk. I wished I could explain to the authorities: 'The people here are traumatized—and you want me to stick a pamphlet on their door telling them their house is in an evacuation zone? Your intention is good, but you don't get it.'

"Johnson's Landing belongs to its residents; it represents their home, identity, culture and way of life; everything they know and love is there. People had already suffered a massive shock. If you turn up in a uniform and try to enforce an evacuation, people will be mortified and some will be angry. I was being pulled in two directions, but I tried to be sensitive."

Bob Yetter certainly appreciated the considerate way in which Chris informed him, on Friday morning, "You're being evacuated—but you don't *have* to leave! I can't *make* you leave, but I just need you to know you *are* in the evacuation zone."

Chris continued: "I was in Johnson's Landing for about seven days. My organization [the RCMP] was happy to say they had someone there on the ground on the stranded side, but they had little resource at first to assist me in my duties. The Landing residents were wonderful and we bonded. They made sure I had everything I needed, and more, even produce from their gardens. I stayed with Tony Holland, a retired RCMP officer, then moved to Clint Carlson's cabin above the beach after that area was deemed safe.

"There was a camaraderie, a sense that we were in this together for the next little while. I picked up on the minor strife between different personalities—certain people definitely chafed against one another. But people put aside their differences and came together in an inspiring way, to get through this as best they could. For example, we worked together taking turns to water Patrick Steiner's farm after the family had evacuated.

"I bathed in the lake each evening, washed my uniform with shampoo and hung it to dry on the beach. One evening I was bathing, nude, when around the bay came this media boat. Oh Jesus! I'm in the lake with nothing on, and my uniform is hanging in a tree! I kept my head down, hoping they'd hurry up and leave before they noticed and filmed me for the evening news!

"Once the recovery was under way, I had to inform Kaslo headquarters when human remains were discovered. By law I was the one to notify the coroner and keep continuity of the body till the coroner made a decision. Those days—when we found Val and Diana—weren't easy. I coordinated transporting the bodies off the site. As a police officer I was used to dealing with death, but this was different—a tragedy affecting the whole community that I felt very much a member of by that time.

"They were long days—eighteen hours sometimes. When I finally got back to Kaslo I was exhausted. I'd been isolated for a whole week, unaware that everyone in Kaslo was also affected. I hadn't realized how the youth were grieving for Rachel and Diana. With no access to TV, I'd missed seeing how the story was reported and, of course, that video footage of the second slide. I watched in amazement and thought, 'Wow! I was in Bob Yetter's house when that thing flushed out.'

"The Johnson's Landing landslide was the first time in my professional career that tragedy had hit *my* community. Elsewhere I was just a cop doing his job, depersonalized and objective. But this disaster resonated with me. In my Canadian policing career this was the biggest event I'd ever attended as an emergency responder, and the first natural disaster I ever saw. I'll never forget it.

"I said my goodbyes and left Kaslo for the last time on Labour Day. The people gave me so much over those three years, and I was glad I could do something for them when they needed my professionalism the most."

Bruce Walker, Manager, Kaslo Search and Rescue

Bruce Walker became involved in Search and Rescue (SAR) in his early twenties, through his interest and expertise in rock climbing and rope-work rescue. He was chair of the Mountain Rescue training project for BC during the 1980s and a provincial instructor for rope rescue; he's taught the skill to most of the SAR groups in the southeastern interior of BC. Bruce and a friend have a private company that runs rescue training courses for industry, which include advice on setting up teams, best practices, gear and equipment, and training the trainers.

Bruce is one of five managers of Kaslo Search and Rescue, a non-profit society in which everyone volunteers their time. SAR encompasses disciplines such as ground search and rescue, swift water rescue, rope rescue and mountain rescue.

On July 12 Bruce learned about the landslide from Chris Backus, and asked his SAR colleague Paddy Flanagan to respond. Bruce remained in Kaslo to relay Paddy's needs. Communication out of Johnson's Landing was problematic from the beginning.

Paddy Flanagan left Kaslo immediately with Stefan Letrari. The immensity of the disaster hit them as they drove north and looked across the lake. "What is a clear-cut like that doing in Johnson's Landing?" Paddy asked. When they arrived, geotechnical expert Peter Jordan advised Paddy that a second landslide was extremely likely. Nobody was permitted to enter the debris area, but Paddy had great difficulty restraining the local emergency responders who wanted to go in and start searching, regardless of the danger.

Paddy quickly concluded that the landslide was beyond the scope of the local SAR. Bruce and Paddy thought initially that the rescue operation might require specialist equipment Kaslo did not have, to cut into mangled buildings and concrete basements. Only later did Bruce realize that their own local expertise in avalanche searches was one of their greatest assets. "It became evident that this was like an avalanche search where you could not probe, and no one was wearing a transceiver." Bruce and his team were on more familiar territory than they had first realized.

Bruce contacted the Heavy Urban Search and Rescue (HUSAR) task force in Vancouver, a special operations team of up to a hundred and twenty members with medical, fire suppression, emergency response, search and rescue, and engineering backgrounds. The task force rescues victims from major structural collapses and other hazards. Vancouver's is one of four national HUSAR teams able to deploy anywhere in Canada, and the only Canadian team certified to be deployed internationally by the coordinator for the United Nations Emergency Response program.

HUSAR sent an initial response team of five people by chartered plane on Thursday afternoon. They assessed the scene, reported back to Vancouver Thursday night and initiated a full-scale response on Friday morning. Fifty-five personnel and two transport truckloads of gear and communications equipment arrived in Kaslo on Friday afternoon and deployed to Johnson's Landing to assess the debris field.

Bruce Walker, in his role as incident commander, set up the SAR command centre at the Kaslo Arena. Communications between Johnson's Landing and the outside world were extremely difficult. There was no cellphone coverage in the Landing, and even HUSAR's communications equipment did not work there. For several days they used the 911 emergency repeater at the Trail fire department, until they obtained blue channel radios used by the Ministry of Forests.

Another headache for Bruce was transportation. They needed medium-sized helicopters, but many were away fighting the first of that summer's wildfires. The best he could find were A-Star five-seaters, which could carry only two or three passengers at a time, plus their equipment.

Bruce had to ensure that the rescue task force dug carefully, in accordance with Bob Stair's methodology. Bob's expertise in excavating grave and burial sites was crucial, and he would soon be taking command of the recovery operation.

Bruce stayed in Kaslo as the go-to person for HUSAR: the one who knew how to obtain what they needed and make things happen. He got barely two hours' sleep a night between Thursday and Sunday. On Saturday, July 14, and Sunday, July 15, one hundred and fourteen search and rescue personnel (from twenty-two agencies) were on-site. Bruce went to Johnson's Landing himself on Saturday to help Bob Stair locate the Webber and Frehse houses.

Local residents Eric Schindler and Zan Mautner helped Bruce find the site of Petra Frehse's former cabin. Eric knew exactly where Petra's cabin lay, but when he tried to get over there to offer his assistance, the guards at the Rogers Road roadblock on the north side of Gar Creek refused—for two full days—to let him pass. Eric, a mild-mannered, soft-spoken man with snowy white hair and beard, was beside himself with frustration as other volunteers and first responders were waved through the barricade. He pleaded with the police, "If young Kaslo SAR guys can go in, surely I can. I am seventy-four years old, and if I get killed over there it doesn't matter as much."

Only late on Saturday afternoon was Eric finally allowed through the barricade, with Gerry Rogers. They had to promise not to go beyond Roger and Carol's house, one hundred metres down the road, but they ignored the instruction and went on to the command post near the Webber house. Bruce Walker and Bob Stair greeted Eric enthusiastically—they'd been given his name as a resource person. Eric was exasperated: "I'd been pushing so desperately for two days to get through the roadblock. Now they were glad to see me!"

Light was fading fast and nothing more could be done that day. Eric returned on Sunday morning with Zan Mautner, the son of Petra's close friend Edith, who has first responder training. This time Eric had an official permit and a vehicle to meet him (the Corix smart meter installer's truck, which SAR was now using). Eric and Zan took about an hour and a half to identify the spot where Petra's cabin lay buried, and Bruce confirmed via GPS that they were right on target.

When Bruce stepped down as incident commander and handed authority to Lisa Lapointe, BC's chief coroner, Bob Stair became the site commander on the ground. On Sunday afternoon, with the mission reclassified as a "recovery" and the BC Coroners Service in charge, the SAR teams from around the province, including HUSAR, stepped down.

The operation now required only six to eight people doing excavation work. Twenty-four members of HUSAR stayed on as safety personnel—controlling the road access and acting as spotters for the excavation team.

Bruce oversaw the four-day excavation at Petra's. The house lay buried very deeply and time ran out before they could make much headway moving the mountain of material that covered it. In reality there was far more likelihood of success at the Webbers' than at Petra's.

In November 2012, Bruce Walker was awarded the Queen's Diamond Jubilee Medal for his significant contribution as Kaslo's SAR manager to the search and recovery efforts after the Johnson's Landing landslides, particularly in coordinating equipment, accommodation, transportation, food, water and information to the other involved agencies.

Bob Stair, Former BC Coroner and Forensic Anthropology Specialist

On Friday morning Bruce Walker requested assistance from Bob Stair, a retired coroner who lives in Kaslo. Bob's first task was intelligence gathering, and by ten a.m. he was in a helicopter hovering above the bay at Johnson's Landing, examining the scene. He was perfectly placed to observe a small motorboat that cruised the shoreline and landed near the mouth of Gar Creek. He recalls saying to the pilot, "What are those stupid people doing down there?" with no idea that one of them was his friend and mountain climbing buddy Osa Thatcher.

Observing movement on the hillside the helicopter veered away up the creek channel, giving Bob a bird's-eye view of the second mudslide as it erupted in great surges that resembled in texture a snow avalanche. Wave upon wave of mud began sweeping down the gulley.

During his twenty-six-year career with the RCMP, Bob had returned to school to study forensic anthropology and become a specialist in the investigation of burials, graves, scattered remains, mass fatalities and missing persons. He'd worked closely with the BC Coroners Service, and when he left the RCMP in 1996 the Coroners Service asked him to join them.

At first he worked only in Canada, but he was increasingly called on to assist foreign governments, the United Nations and non-governmental organizations with overseas investigations. These included searching for World War II Gestapo graves in the Ukraine; the excavation of mass graves in Kosovo and East Timor; and humanitarian recovery missions in the war-torn northern Tamil region of Sri Lanka.

Back in Canada in 2002, Bob helped oversee a massive forensic investigation of the Robert William Pickton farm near Vancouver, BC, where an unknown number of missing women were believed buried. He assisted in designing the forensic process for the Pickton investigation after visiting the site of the World Trade Center in New York, and learning from the recovery operation carried out there after the 9/11 attack in 2001. Bob was also the technical consultant to the hugely popular Canadian television drama series *Da Vinci's Inquest*, which explored the career of a fictional BC coroner.

Bob developed a methodology for best practice in excavation technique that is widely recognized and used today. His first mantra is: "Don't worry about the bodies. If you do a good job of excavating, and you manage the material correctly, your reward will be the bodies." Tempting though it might be, it is crazy to simply dig a five-metre hole in a likely area and expect to find something. This approach creates an outflow of material piled up around the hole. If the hole leads nowhere, then all that dug material must be moved a second time. "Only move the dirt once!" is his second mantra.

Bob was certain that the four victims of Thursday's landslide were no longer alive. This would be a recovery, not a rescue. While Bob waited for authorization to take charge of the operation, he and his team used Google maps and GPS satellite measurements to pinpoint the locations of the Frehse and Webber houses. Local residents provided diagrams and photographs of the houses, and Bob requested information about the people inside. Where were they believed to be? When had they last been seen or spoken to?

The digging began initially at the Webber residence, and the Frehse property was addressed as more equipment arrived. Petra Frehse's house had been buried under about eight metres of debris, whereas the Webber property was under three metres.

An excavator, Bob's tool of choice, is highly efficient and the Kootenay Lake valley is fortunately full of them, along with skilled operators. Excavator operators are generally "production" oriented, however, and Bob needed to coach them in the unfamiliar realm of excavating for bodies. He instructed them to go slowly and carefully, skimming the surface and taking it very easy. An operation of this kind requires restraint and discipline and excellent communication between the excavator operator and those who are watching the bucket and material outflow.

Bob is accustomed to seeing human remains, but needed to pay attention to the civilians around him and prepare them for what would happen if they found a body. People were admittedly scared, not knowing how they themselves might react. Bob strongly sang the praises of all the operators and team members for their remarkable skill and willingness to adapt their methods to this new task.

Workers' safety was a constant concern and the HUSAR personnel provided excellent site security. Frequent safety drills required everyone to run to "safe zones." This chewed into the day and could be frustrating, but was a necessary adjunct to the work. Spotters and safety personnel watched the upper hillside, ready to sound air horns if anything moved.

The chief coroner was acutely concerned about the risk of another landslide that could lead to further injuries or deaths among the workers. There were also budgetary constraints. Lisa Lapointe gave Bob four full days to conduct his search for the bodies. On Sunday, July 15, they found Val Webber's body, and the next day they found his daughter Diana. The search was suspended on Wednesday, July 18. As mentioned earlier, the stoppage met with fierce opposition and criticism from some in the Johnson's Landing and Kaslo communities.

Behind the scenes over the next week Bob talked with Lisa Lapointe, confident that he could find Rachel, given just two more days. He drew up a budget, initially discouraged by the high cost. Workplace BC safety standards are rigorous, requiring, for example, an ambulance on-site with two crew members—which alone would eat up half Bob's budget. But the Kaslo community was determined to get the recovery effort underway again. The SAR team and other key people offered their time and the budget began to look more reasonable. The chief coroner gave Bob the okay on Monday, July 23. They found Rachel Webber's body at around six p.m. on Wednesday, July 25, a short distance away from her father and sister.

Despite his long years of experience disinterring human remains, Bob found this recovery operation difficult because, for the first time, he was among members of his own community. Although he hadn't known the victims personally he knew many people who'd been close to them. Bob was both touched and disturbed, and found himself thinking a lot about Val, Diana, Rachel and Petra. The personal reaction was reassuring. Empathy and sensitivity were luxuries he could not allow himself in his long career as a clinically detached "death professional." Bob is glad he could employ his special area of expertise to be of assistance to his community, and is deeply appreciative of the team members who worked alongside him.

In January 2013, Bob Stair was awarded the Queen's Diamond Jubilee Medal in a ceremony in Vancouver. Premier Christy Clark presented the medal in recognition of Bob's outstanding leadership and public service to BC communities.

Deb Borsos, Recovery Manager

Deb's background, training, interests and aptitudes, as well as her local knowledge and networking panache, made her an ideal candidate for a very daunting job. Her energy and sense of humour didn't hurt either.

Deb was born in the Okanagan and raised in the Fraser Valley, in southwestern BC. Her mother, a Quaker, worked as a nurse, and her father was an art teacher. Hers was a creative family of painters, potters, filmmakers and multimedia artists, and Deb herself specializes in pastel landscapes.

Deb attended the Quaker Friends School in Argenta, which she calls "the best thing that ever happened to me: I took a left turn and never looked back." She graduated in 1979 and went travelling the world. In 1982 she spent a year in Argenta finishing her studies for a diploma in horticulture. Thirteen years later she reconnected with Argenta friend Rik Valentine, and they've been together ever since. They moved back to Argenta in the winter of 1996, arriving just before Christmas. Rik called up Vince McIntyre, a local farmer, hoping to buy some winter vegetables, and Deb remembers Vince's arrival, through deep snow, with his horse and sleigh, tinkling with bells. As well as potatoes he brought them a bottle of whisky. It was a fine homecoming.

Deb developed an interest in emergency recovery management, partly because Rik is the fire warden for the area and Deb was accustomed to listening to the fire radio and monitoring wildfires. She is one of three dispatchers for Argenta's Emergency Preparedness Team and became Argenta and North Kootenay Lake's representative on the

RDCK's Area D Emergency Planning Committee in 2006. When the Johnson's Landing landslides occurred, Deb was partway through a study course for certification as an emergency manager, offered through the Justice Institute of BC. She has since qualified.

Deb learned about the first slide from Gail Spitler, about ten minutes after it happened. Just that morning Deb had received an email informing her that the RDCK's emergency manager, Noreen Clayton, was now on vacation. In the event of an emergency, Deb was to contact Noreen's backup in the East Kootenay. Deb tried to locate the backup, then called the Provincial Emergency Centre in Victoria. Hers was the second call reporting the event, made after Bob Yetter's 911 call.

Deb gave the operator the scant details she had. When she added "and there might be houses buried under the landslide..." the tone at the other end of the line changed. Communications systems snapped into action. Fire, police and ambulance were alerted, and Deb was impressed to hear the sirens approaching on the highway across the lake less than half an hour later.

Deb spent the first week post-slide in Kaslo, assisting the ESS team at the reception centre. She saw the devastation for the first time on July 18 when she flew to the Landing and helped coordinate a meeting between the Red Cross and the remaining residents. On July 23, Deb was offered the job of recovery manager for the Johnson's Landing landslide disaster. The RDCK intimated that she might be in the post till October 2012, but Deb was at work until July 2014. This disaster was unusual, and a number of issues still remained unresolved two years later.

Her job description included serving as a liaison with the community of Johnson's Landing regarding their needs; sharing information with them; serving on the Unmet Needs Committee; assisting with grant applications; learning the Disaster Financial Assistance (DFA) manual inside and out;

liaising with the DFA representative; and working with the Multi-Agency Recovery Team (MRT).

Falling under the Provincial Emergency Program of Emergency Management BC (EMBC), Disaster Financial Assistance is a funding program that provides financial assistance to individuals when catastrophic events have resulted in uninsurable property and infrastructure damage. DFA provides assistance to replace or restore items that are essential to one's home, livelihood or community service. Deb worked with Tim MacLeod from the DFA Program for a full year. She found him to be a creative and imaginative individual. "He tries to take the DFA manual, turn it on its head and still make it work—which is exactly what that job should entail. He advocated for the clients, hated saying no, and really wanted to help. Tim is an excellent person for that job and we were lucky to have him." Deb, for her part, ensured that Tim had every scrap of applicable information relevant to the Johnson's Landing DFA claimants.

The MRT was born from a simple idea broached by Hugh Eberle of the Ministry of Transportation and Infrastructure (MOTI): that all ministries and agencies connected with the disaster recovery should sit down at the same table once a fortnight. Participants included the Ministry of Forests, various RDCK personnel, BC Hydro, MOTI, BC Parks and geotechnical expert Doug Nicol. The agency representatives brainstormed, discussed ongoing matters and offered mutual assistance.

Deb provided community information to help the MRT do its job better. She pointed out on one occasion that Johnson's Landing is home to an unusual bunch of people, many of them highly educated, independent-minded, opinionated and unlikely to share similar opinions on more than a few topics. This fact made the work continually interesting, and Deb's observation offered the MRT perspective as they discussed options for ongoing recovery matters.

Deb loves dealing with a hundred things at once—she is a natural multi-tasker. She carried forward the conversations, answered questions, and connected people with the information and forms they needed. It was reminiscent of her earlier career as a ward clerk in hospital emergency rooms in Vancouver and Victoria. "This job was such an opportunity, though I feel guilty saying it. It's horrible in one sense to see disaster as an opportunity, but it was, and I hope I can use the knowledge I gained to help others in future with their recoveries."

Her toughest task? Sending out the information bulletins that kept the community apprised of events. Somebody, inevitably, would be offended, though Deb took great pains with the wording. Regular community updates were essential. They were the glue that kept the community connected, especially for people who'd been forced to leave the Landing and now lived elsewhere.

How did Deb deal with criticism? "I decided that this job wasn't 'mine' to own, and I took a neutral position. This was a hugely traumatic event for people and if they reacted to me critically I understood and didn't take it personally. Most of the people in Johnson's Landing have been amazing, absolutely wonderful."

Deb is writing a recovery manager's manual she hopes will fill a knowledge gap and assist in training new recovery managers. It's a how-to-do-it guide with examples of how to support people and assist their recovery in small, rural or remote communities. Deb would advise any prospective recovery manager to, at a minimum:

1. Take training in psychosocial trauma counselling. Deb saw the effects of trauma in people but didn't always know how best to help them: "I was afraid I would say or do the wrong thing." And she recognized symptoms of that same trauma in herself, because of everything she saw and heard.

2. Understand the Disaster Financial Assistance manual.
3. Know and understand the Incident Command System used by Emergency Management BC (EMBC).

EMBC has a clear chain of command structure, which is necessary in order to be effective in emergency events. This, in Deb's estimation, can lead to a provision of services that, when used in a small or remote community that is normally very independent in its actions, feels like it's being done *to* you rather than *for* you. There is good reason for responders to act according to the set command structure, primarily for safety reasons, but in the case of Johnson's Landing, it did not match the priorities of the affected residents.

Someday, she'd love to see the organizational chart used in emergency events include a community liaison from the affected community, just to have a direct source of local knowledge available as soon as possible to help the responders. The current chart employs a liaison officer, tasked with contacting the school district, fire department and so on, but that person does not necessarily have direct connections to local residents. But Deb is also a realist. She hopes in time to see a greater meshing of the two approaches, but accepts that change may take some time.

As her job wound down and she contemplated what would come next, Deb drew inspiration from the new trees planted in the landslide as part of the Regrowth Project, intended to help stabilize portions of the slide area. Spring 2013 saw them put out their first leaves and by the early summer of 2014 they were still doing well. Deb took a photo, and commented, "Life is coming back! I love that photo! It will be the cover of my manual."

Duncan Lake, Excavator Operator

Duncan has lived most of his life at the north end of Kootenay Lake. His grandparents, Stanley and Ethel Lake, were among the first white settlers in Johnson's Landing in the 1920s, and Duncan's dad, Roy, was born and raised in the Landing. As a young man, Duncan worked as a tree planter: "I planted a million trees before I ever did any logging!" He later bought two excavators and learned the skills of machine logging.

On July 12, 2012, Duncan was in Nelson, working on a house porch, assisted by his daughter, Andrea. They heard the news on CBC Radio and Andrea, a friend of Rachel Webber, was greatly concerned. She'd spoken to Rachel in the Landing only that morning, and knew the family was there. Duncan and Andrea drove back to Kaslo and went to the house Rachel was renting with Zoei Thibault. A group of distraught high school friends had gathered there and Duncan, together with several other parents, took care of the young people through Thursday and Friday as the news bulletins grew ever more pessimistic.

Duncan was frustrated, eager to get busy and help the rescue effort. His connection to the Landing was profound, and he knew the Webbers slightly—he'd logged their land a few years back. He was relieved when Bruce Walker called him on Sunday to request his assistance in looking for Petra. Duncan's Hyundai machine was smaller than some, and better suited to the difficult terrain close to the site of Petra's cabin.

Duncan dug down to ground level at Petra's, a depth of about eight metres. "The cabin had exploded into shards and was spread on the ground over a large area," he told me. Stan Baker and Duncan switched places on Tuesday, because Stan's machine was bigger, and more able to cope with the vast volume of material that had to be shifted. Duncan assisted Bob Stair at the Webbers' house site, until the recovery operation halted.

He was back there with Bob when the excavation work resumed the following week. "It was so hard to figure out where we were; no one could get a good picture. The roof had moved one way, the washer another, the hot water tank in a third direction—entropy, I guess." Duncan uncovered and set aside a number of valuable mementos such as Diana's quote book, her camera and a suitcase of her clothes. But after Rachel's body was recovered, the excavators quickly closed the site in, burying everything.

Duncan realizes now that he, Bob and others on the team made a wrong assumption: "We felt it was a favour to Lynn to not have to see the house debris, and not have to deal with it. We thought the stuff should maybe stay buried, and everyone assumed this was what Lynn wanted." But when she found out, Lynn called Duncan in great distress. "It transpired that what we were doing was in complete contradiction with what she wanted—she wanted to salvage much more." Lynn had hoped to extract the roof and many good, usable timbers that could have created a new structure, and she wanted to search for meaningful things in the wreckage.

Duncan assisted many of us over those first weeks. He created roadways across the slide to the Madills' house and to Harvey's, which was very difficult because of the many huge trees driven deep into the mud. At the request of Eric Schindler, Duncan placed a memorial rock on the remaining corner of Petra's land. And, of course, he worked with Christopher on the excavation of our house. On the basis of his experience digging at the Webbers', Duncan was not confident that we would find very much, and was unsure whether such an excavation was a good idea. "It was kind of a beautiful spot, smooth and polished off, with wonderful views all around. I thought it would have been nice to just leave it alone." However, he was astounded by the quantity of valuable things Christopher extracted. "I thought that finding your car would be a stretch, but it was the first thing we hit."

The following October, working on the trench from Gerry Rogers's property to Moss Beard Spring, Duncan undertook his scariest excavation work, during torrential rain—the first deluge since early July. "The air was gaseous, coming out of the dirt almost like foam in places. The surface looked like a soup. If I tossed a rock into the material it was gone, submerged, like in a quicksand. That project was probably the most dangerous thing I did."

The landslides have left Duncan with two enduring thoughts. "I observe landscape with new eyes now, and often see places where people should not have built houses. It's crazy!" The second is a new intolerance for any television programs that involve "people being mean to one another; I cannot watch that kind of thing anymore."

I'D LIKE TO end this chapter by acknowledging the bravery of Stan Baker, a very experienced excavator operator, who took great personal risks in his determination to cross the slide and make his machine available for what everyone still hoped would be a dig for rescue.

Stan trucked his enormous CAT 320 into Johnson's Landing on Thursday, July 12, in the afternoon, walked it down the road to Creek Corner and began removing debris. Approaching the mud he clawed at a big log, put it down in front of him and looked for more, wanting to distribute the load and weight of the "twenty-ton hoe" by creating a float-like corduroy road across the muck and mire.

Almost at once he bogged down and began to sink, with the mud reaching a quarter of the way up his cab door. He couldn't swing to the right or use the bucket. And now his only exit from the cab was through the escape window at the back. "It was not a very good situation," he told me afterwards, with characteristic understatement. But he stayed calm and kept swinging to the left, pushing mud, until he could turn completely around and lift himself out of the soup. Some would have retreated to safety at this point, but Stan persevered, wanting only to go forward and reach the south side.

Johnnie Command, a colleague in another excavator, began passing wood to Stan. Johnnie gave Stan enough material to support the colossal weight as the hoe inched its way to the middle of the creek draw, where some water gushed and the mud was pudding soft. Stan grabbed logs, laid them down and, about an hour after he'd started, got his machine grounded safely on the other side, just as daylight was beginning to fail.

Stan parked his excavator for the night up by the Fry Creek trailhead, then went home to Kaslo. He returned the next morning, ready to start digging. At ten a.m. he was standing by his machine at the trailhead, recounting his adventures to Bob Yetter, when the second landslide thundered down, sweeping away the corduroy road and everything else in its path.

Stan Baker's CAT, moments before it became bogged down while Stan attempted to cross the slide at Creek Corner on Thursday evening, July 12.

Chapter 11: Earth and Water

ARGENTINE NOVELIST AND poet Julio Cortázar once wrote that he may have been too trusting in *"la fiel caricia de mi tierra"*—"the faithful caress of my land." In a similar vein, many of us in Johnson's Landing perhaps allowed ourselves to be beguiled into believing that our mountain actually cared about us. Every evening Kootenay Joe Ridge exhaled a fragrant downdraft of warm air that sent smoke and sparks from our beach fire out across the lake. In the soft light of morning a perceptible breath of cool air rose from the water, crossed the meadow and floated up the hill as the mountain inhaled. We loved our mountain; it seemed a benign protector, sheltering us and nurturing our needs with its living waters. Blinded by the conviction that I would always be safe under Kootenay Joe Ridge, maybe that's why I failed to heed the signs—the changes in the creek, the odd smell, even Loran's emails.

Of course, it's easy to see now that, besides being exhausted from my trip to England and saddened by my mother's declining state, I was thinking like a child, lulled by the naïve temptation to anthropomorphize a lump of rock. Adam Gopnik, on BBC Radio 4's *A Point of View*, once described this kind of magical thinking: "We had faith in the benevolence of the universe, in a compact the world had made with us that all things turn out well." But adult truth sweeps that trust away, as Gopnik goes on to explain:

"The world makes no compacts with you at all. You can only hope to negotiate a short-term treaty, or armistice, which the world, like a half-mad monarch, will then break, just as it likes."

The mountain above Johnson's Landing is neither good nor bad; it does not love, hate, protect or neglect us. The world moves forward through time and space, indifferent to the life it carries on its rounded back, oblivious to our prayers, opinions or dogma.

We in the Landing drew comfort from the history of uneventful habitation since Algot Johnson bought the first acreage on the hillside in 1906—a fraction of a nano-second ago in the lifespan of Kootenay Lake. No natural disasters had befallen Johnson's Landing in our modern history apart from a few nearby forest fires and the occasional snow avalanche partway down Gar Creek. People relaxed in a false sense of security. False, because the mountain *has* moved before, several times, in the distant past. And Gar Creek has been the conduit for other floods and debris flows. The signs were visible if you knew how to find them.

Peter Jordan, a geotechnical expert with the Ministry of Forests, told us that he'd identified an ancient landslide path on Kootenay Joe Ridge, much larger than the 2012 slide, and two smaller, more recent slide paths. His team used light detection and ranging (LIDAR) equipment, which gives an accurate map of the surface topography as if no trees were present. These telltale scars, dating from a period more than 12,000 years ago, were invisible until modern technology enabled scientists to scrutinize the forest floor beneath the dense canopy of trees.

Our beach at the mouth of Gar Creek, it transpired, also held evidence of prehistoric events—an alluvial fan created by previous debris flows and floods. In a 1998 report to the Ministry of Water, Land and Air Protection entitled *Terrain Stability Inventory, Alluvial and Debris Torrent Fans, Kootenay Region*, the Gar Creek fan was identified as a potential debris flow area. And in 2004 it was noted as such on Ministry of Environment flood hazard maps.

In 2009 the Regional District of Central Kootenay (RDCK) described the Gar Creek fan as a "Non-Standard Flood and Erosion Polygon area" in its Floodplain Management Bylaw No. 2080. But they didn't share this information; they didn't tell us, the people who lived there. The RDCK didn't make the information public or readily accessible, so that we, living in the middle of this "non-standard flood and erosion polygon area," had no idea there might be a potential hazard. Had we applied for a building permit it would likely have been refused on grounds of flood and debris flow risk.

I wonder if I would have reacted differently if I had been aware of our home's precarious location. If I'd read published reports and registered, even subconsciously, the phrases "debris flow hazard" and "flood risk," I wonder if I would have responded with alarm to the indicators I observed in Gar Creek on Tuesday, Wednesday and Thursday morning—the stink, the turbid water that became a mud slurry, the exceptionally high flow.

If I'd known, would I have leapt up, heart racing, and grabbed Ozzie, phoned Jillian, asked to use their truck to carry stuff to Kaslo? Would I have alerted Renata and told her, "You can't stay here, it isn't safe," and loaded some of my bags into her car? If I had known, would I have...? These sorts of questions and scenarios torment the survivors of any catastrophe. The anguish can be agonizing, because we always think we *should* have known.

In 2012, however, no central repository for known hazard information existed for our area. After the slide, the geotechnical experts recommended in their report to the RDCK that "Residents and the general public should be made aware of and/or understand how to access existing landslide hazard information, new landslide reports and new landslide hazard maps."

The long-awaited final geotechnical report was made public at a meeting in Argenta on May 23, 2013. *RDCK: Johnson's Landing Landslide Hazard and Risk Assessment* was commissioned by the RDCK, and paid for by the provincial government. The report's findings were devastating to us all, but particularly to certain property owners in the Landing.

The risk of another landslide was such that parts of Johnson's Landing are unacceptably dangerous for human habitation and can never be reoccupied. There is a one in ten risk in any given year that a landslide will occur in the area of the Gar Creek channel and alluvial fan. The report rates eighteen private properties at risk from landslides in the future. Five properties are in a very high hazard zone, rated 1:10 to 1:100; nine properties lie in a 1:100 to 1:1,000 (high) hazard zone; and four properties are in a 1:1,000 to 1:10,000 (moderate) hazard zone. The main road into Johnson's Landing, where it crosses Gar Creek, and the public road down to the beach are in a high hazard zone. As a result, the Ministry of Transportation and Infrastructure closed the lower portion of the beach access road in 2013.

The report called the Johnson's Landing landslide "unprecedented in recent history in this region with respect to its large size." Only three other known landslides of a similar order of magnitude have occurred across southern British Columbia—all of them since 1999. And climate change projections for the Kootenay region do not bode well for the future.

What triggered this landslide? The ground water table was very high, for one thing, and that reduced the effective strength of the soil. And the rainfall in June 2012 was record-breaking, a one-in-a-hundred-year event. The snowpack on the mountains that winter was also heavier than usual. Then, incredibly, a week before the landslide, the weather turned dry and sunny. How could a weather change, which seemed so marvellous when I returned from grey, dismal London, wreak such havoc?

That week temperatures rose to over thirty degrees Celsius. While I lay basking on the deck, watching the swallows, the abrupt heat wave hastened the snowmelt, which seeped underground through the porous limestone and emerged as springs that fed a boggy area at the slide source. Saturated from above, this deep pocket of material was also inundated from below. During that week Gar Creek was flowing at possibly its highest level in forty years. The snowpack, the deluge of rain and the heat wave: three ingredients in a recipe for disaster.

And the future? The technical information is complicated for the layman, hard to comprehend, because it involves projections based on risk factors found during post-slide searches. The geotechnical team found fractures and tension cracks, aquifers and springs that might, over time, weaken the soil. And apparently a potentially unstable volume of glacial and colluvial deposits. At the time of the first landslide, a block of earth and debris dropped twenty metres then stopped, possibly held in place by bedrock. This "intact block" is considered likely to form future landslides, small or large.

In their report, the geotechnical team calculated the risk of a 50,000-cubic-metre landslide at 1:50, and a 96,000-cubic-metre slide at 1:100. A future landslide of similar magnitude to the 2012 slide (320,000 cubic metres), unimpeded by trees, might extend farther across the Johnson's Landing bench. Of course, there are unknown factors. Will the unstable earth move again? Will extreme weather caused by climate change increase groundwater levels?

Christopher and I sat in the meeting, sombre and concerned. I looked around the room, at Osa and Paul, Loran and Gerry, Jillian and John, Kate and Harvey. Our faces were blank, our minds reeling in the pieces of information that we could most readily grasp. Few of us had been given an opportunity to read the 102-page report before the meeting.

Eleven recommendations included increasing the height of the ridge at the bend in Gar Creek near Petra Frehse's property, establishing a simple landslide monitoring program, and creating communication plans and protocols to update residents and visitors about local conditions during periods of increased landslide hazard. Those times of greatest danger will likely be the wettest months: June and October. The report also recommended restricting residential development in moderate, high or very high hazard zones.

We looked at each other in despair.

THE RISK ANALYSIS left property owners like the Madills, Harvey Armstrong and Rachel Rozzoni in a quandary. Large tracts of their properties were now uninhabitable and could not be used for any purpose. Yet, and here's the rub, they remain the legal owners, and liable for the land. Although property taxes and insurance still had to be paid, the land was virtually valueless and unsellable. How could this be?

Insurance companies refused to honour home insurance policies on the grounds that landslides and land subsidence (the ground giving way) are excluded from coverage. Faced with this horror, it seemed reasonable to everyone, especially those caught in the trap, to hope that the provincial government would expropriate the land of the three or four most affected residents, provide some fair compensation and revert it to the Crown. But no such offer was made.

Harvey Armstrong, for instance, lost the use of most of his land and all the buildings. The property lies in a total exclusion zone, with a 1:1,000 risk of being impacted by another landslide. He told me, "It used to be worth $200,000 and now it's worth nothing. But that's not the worst of it. The worst is I am still the owner and I am liable if someone goes onto my land and gets hurt. I get sued. So I must have liability insurance. And I'm still paying taxes." If the landslides had been a one-off event, Harvey could have continued to use his land. But the potential for another landslide puts him in limbo.

Rachel Rozzoni and Dan Tarini had house insurance on their property, but the insurance company refused to cover their loss. After Rachel was forced to evacuate, the insurance premium leapt from $2,600 to $4,000 per year *because the house was standing empty.* "We paid our premiums for nearly ten years," she said. "They [the insurance company] could have given us back that last year's premium, but they didn't help us, or even make a donation as a sign of goodwill." From the Disaster Financial Assistance (DFA) program, Rachel and Dan received 80 percent of the value of their house (excluding land and outbuildings), conditional on the building being demolished, which it was.

The Madills did not receive "a dime" from their insurance company either. And DFA provided only limited compensation. "It's intended as a hand-up, but it doesn't lift you up very far because things cost a lot," Jillian said. The DFA program fails rural property owners because the land itself is a major asset. The Madills received no compensation for their outbuildings, workshop, tools, guesthouse and seven hectares of land, three of which now lie under the landslide.

The DFA program has paid out about $578,000 to Johnson's Landing claimants but the program has shortcomings and has been criticized as not suited to the needs of rural communities. Despite BC being a predominantly rural province, the DFA rules give the appearance of having been designed with urban residential environments as the point of reference.

John Kettle, chair of the RDCK, agrees that Johnson's Landing property owners have been placed in an untenable position. Through no fault of their own, owing to a hazard emanating from Crown land, they have lost the ability to use or develop their properties. The situation is unique. No legislation exists to properly address it. In October 2013, Kettle sent a letter to Lori Wanamaker, the chief operating officer of the BC provincial government. In part he wrote:

In my opinion we can and must do better than this. Additionally, with the apparent climate change, this may very well be just the beginning of adverse weather related events throughout the province. God help us if we don't learn and adapt from the Johnson's Landing disaster. This horrible event should be the benchmark by which applicable legislation is generated to address all of the ambiguities and legal nuances we have confronted over the past 15 months. This is not about money but about how we as elected officials, tasked with protecting the public interest and lives, address the reality of climate change for future catastrophic events in British Columbia.

Kettle argued for new provincial legislation to establish a BC Disaster Relief Fund that would compensate residents for their losses (redress of mortgages, taxes, insurance) and recoup the costs incurred as a result of so-called acts of God (evacuation, relocation, etc.). But no such legislation was enacted.

In a letter to residents in December 2013, Kettle explained why the evacuation order for large tracts of Johnson's Landing still remained in force: "With the existence of an unstable scarp containing approximately 800,000 cubic meters of material, and the lack of long-term monitoring data necessary for accurately determining the likelihood of a future landslide… there is an unacceptable risk to life and property associated with occupation of the hazard area at this time."

Kettle renewed the evacuation order weekly for two years, his action reviewed by the Attorney General's office in the Ministry of Justice (the only ministry that could override the RDCK order), and every week they signed off on it. The provincial government and the RDCK also met periodically to discuss issues that remained unresolved.

The RDCK sought long-term solutions from the provincial government prior to lifting the order. In John Kettle's opinion, the 2012 landslides, and the unstable material hanging above the community on Crown land, are the Crown's responsibility, not the RDCK's, and the Ministry of Forests, Lands and Natural Resource Operations (FLNRO) is responsible for implementing the eleven recommendations contained in the geotechnical report. Some believed the provincial government would dearly like to hand these responsibilities to the RDCK and local taxpayers. Two years after the landslide, on July 31, 2014, with most of these issues still unresolved, the evacuation order was finally lifted.

Andy Shadrack, the RDCK director for Johnson's Landing, expressed disappointment: "As far as I'm concerned, the provincial government has absolutely failed the people in Johnson's Landing who, through no fault of their own, lost their houses. If this was somewhere in the Lower Mainland, it would have been settled and the people would have been bought out."

WHEN WILL JOHNSON's Landing's next landslide happen? How bad will it be? Not knowing the answers is, of course, deeply unnerving. When it rains heavily in June and Gar Creek flows fast and turbid, nobody feels entirely safe. What does this uncertainty mean for the future of Johnson's Landing, a community that has lost a quarter of its population through death and displacement? In the aftermath, remaining residents grapple with isolation, loneliness and grief, as well as fear about the future. How do you heal a community that's been told it cannot trust its very environment?

The community began its healing by working together in rebuilding what was destroyed. For the residents on the south (most affected) side of Gar Creek, a vital priority obsessed their waking hours: to re-establish a reliable water source for drinking, domestic use and irrigation.

John Lerbscher spearheaded the various initiatives, and is now an acknowledged community expert on the "water saga." He and his wife, Marlene, bought the old MacNicol pioneer homestead in 1996 and made it their permanent home in 2003. The house stands near Algot Johnson's log house, Harvey Armstrong and Kate O'Keefe's home. Both properties lie safely clear of the landslide and the evacuation zone. John, a chemist by training, is semi-retired from his career as a principal scientist.

In the immediate aftermath of the landslides, John bought a 660-litre water tank and a gas-powered pump, put the tank on an old truck and delivered water to neighbouring households. BC Hydro then stepped in with the donation of a larger tank. But these were just temporary fixes.

The first serious water project was an initiative by Buddy Carlson to replace the water intake in Gar Creek, connecting to a new water distribution box that fed the existing waterlines. Over six ten-hour days, from July 26 to 31, 2012, Sean Brenton and Duncan Lake dug a trench, Bob Yetter and others built a water box, and the Village of Kaslo generously donated a $500 "torpedo"—a specialized serrated pipe, designed to take water out of a creek.

On July 30 and 31, twenty volunteers laid the pipe in the trench and backfilled it by hand, using shovels. Duncan Lake was a key person: courageous and willing to work without hesitation in a high hazard zone; it was just three weeks after the landslides, the creek bank was unstable and no one knew how dangerous the channel might be.

Unfortunately, this first water intake failed after a couple of months. Rocks fell and cracked it, and the unstable creek bank sloughed in, filling the intake with mud.

The second initiative involved an aerial water pipe suspended above the creek, which drew water from Moss Beard Spring on Gerry Rogers's property. Osa Thatcher's son Toby, together with Ruth's grandsons Ed and Will Burt, engineered and constructed the line, which fed the existing water distribution box.

Again, Duncan Lake dug the trench, this time in atrocious weather, with the slide material saturated and slippery. The trench filled with water and the volunteers were soon caked in mud. John said it looked like a scene from a World War I film. It was dangerous work, some would say foolhardy, but the project was completed successfully, and the new line supplied the south-side community's water needs for the next two years. Even though it was intended only as a temporary stopgap, it gave residents breathing space while other, permanent solutions could be considered.

"That spring has been a blessing," John told me, "and we owe Gerry and Linda an ongoing vote of thanks. Despite the disruption it caused to their lives, they have enabled the community to have water, and that's a gift."

The longer-term water saga, however, will be running for some time yet.

The Madills' empty house sits at the edge of the slide area, one year on.

PHOTO: LOUIS BOCKNER

Chapter 12: Calls to Life

The central swath of a landslide is like a giant eraser that removes everything in its path. Houses are buried, trees and landscape obliterated, a moonscape created where every point of reference is gone. When I returned I was bewildered and disorientated. The place had become unrecognizable. Nothing remained for me except the fear that the mountain might move again.

Gail and Lynne and their home have been my bridge back to Johnson's Landing, and my sanctuary on many occasions since July 2012. I always felt safe with them, during a period when I felt unsafe almost everywhere else in the Landing. I'd drive up the lake from Kaslo, thinking positively, intending to visit my derelict garden and see a few friends. Sometimes I got no farther than Gail and Lynne's house. On other occasions I ventured over the creek to the south side but soon returned, distraught.

Invariably, Lynne would make a pot of tea. I'd dry my tears and sit in the flower garden, soothed by watching the birds that flocked to the feeders. Or I'd curl up on their bed for a nap with Tinker the dog, then drive back to Kaslo. It was all right, I would tell myself. I'd return another day to dip my toe in the waters. And so I did, until now, two years on, I cross the slide without too much thought, drive to my friend Kate O'Keefe's house, and revisit the old trails down the hillside that lead to our sad, abandoned garden beside the beach. I carry an old wound, knitted together, that's still tender if I prod it.

In contrast, Christopher chose to spend much of his time in the Landing, and still does, deciding that he would not cut his connections with the place or our friends there. Gail and Lynne are generous employers as well as friends, thoughtful and attentive to the needs of their carpenter. Paul and Osa offer him their house in the Landing—the house the three of them built—and he helps with firewood and building maintenance. His heart lies in Johnson's Landing. I think it always will.

This new arrangement is both a loss and an opportunity. Christopher and I were constant companions during our nineteen years in the Landing. The rhythm of our days embraced walks, boat rides, visiting, team-cooking and gardening, as well as the endless house projects and our local employment commitments. Only my three annual trips to England separated us.

These days, I am alone here in Kaslo for much of the week, until Christopher drives back for a couple of days' R & R. I appreciate our Kaslo home—it's simple and small, with mountain views, minimal gardening chores and easy maintenance. I spend most days quietly engaged in my writing life, thinking, reading and listening to classical music. I volunteer with our hospice society, attend community events and concerts, and have developed a rewarding relationship with our Anglican church. Christopher and I talk daily by phone and email. We honour our time together with bike rides, canoe trips, excursions in the car and special meals. The relationship has certainly evolved, and feels strong as we each answer our respective calls to life.

When someone recently commiserated with me about the disaster, I heard callous-sounding yet honest words coming out of my mouth, words that weren't about the loss of four lives, but about my experience of healing. I said, "Yes, the landslide was a terrible thing, but for me personally it wasn't *all* bad. My life was spared twice in twenty-four hours, and I've been enriched in unexpected ways." I looked at the other person and smiled. We were a large group of locals attending a Kaslo Birdwatchers' potluck supper. The evening was warm, the wine flowed and I enjoyed every bite of the lavish and imaginatively prepared feast.

ANN MACNAB DIED two weeks after the landslides, and in her last days of life gave us and others many gifts. She instructed her executor to let Christopher and me look through her possessions, and pick out replacements for things we'd lost. We drove to Howser one Sunday in late July 2012, and were offered a wealth of sorely needed household items.

On cold winter nights we reach for Ann's gold mohair blanket, spreading it over the deep red duvet with its matching pillowcases and sheets. We sauté potatoes for breakfast in Ann's cast iron skillet and make regular use of many other pots, pans, dishes and utensils from her kitchen. I drink my afternoon tea from her delicate Royal Doulton china mug. The quality of my wardrobe was greatly enriched thanks to the coincidence that Ann and I shared a similar taste in fashion and, amazingly, wore exactly the same size, both in clothes and footwear. From her enormous library we gladly replaced treasured volumes, including the Winnie the Pooh series and many other classics of English and Canadian literature. We placed our new book collection on Ann's Swedish wooden bookshelves. Ann's computer printer has done sterling work delivering hard copies of this manuscript. Countless other fine quality, beautiful things of hers fill in the gaps in our new life. I remember Ann almost every day and feel gratitude.

WE'VE CREATED A photo montage, pinned to a large bulletin board on the kitchen wall, adorned with photos of Ruth's house and its interiors, the creek, the garden, Ozzie, our parents and family. I fall into a reverie gazing at the poignant images of happy times past, and weigh the losses, sensing their heft and pull. These nostalgic mental pilgrimages seem to be an inevitable part of the healing process through grief.

Our photo display includes several pictures of "Teddy," who was lost in the slide. Teddy was Christopher's bear. He was small, no more than eight inches tall, with bright yellow fur and an expressive, handsome face. When I met Christopher on Manitoulin Island for the second time, in 1992, I also met Teddy.

We fell in love that summer. When it was time for me to fly back to England, Christopher gave me a box that I was instructed not to open until I was on the plane. Inside I found Teddy, holding a note that told me he'd like to come along and see London. "Chris" had asked him to keep an eye on me. And it was imperative that I return him safely to Chris as soon as possible.

When we settled into Ruth's house in the Landing, Teddy made himself at home on a shelf in the kitchen, beside storage jars of dried mint, flaked coconut and black peppercorns. He sported a Bahamian shell bracelet round his neck, and a knitted egg cozy as a hat for winter days. Luckily, I took a few photos of him and kept them in Kaslo.

Another photo on our bulletin board shows us in the front yard one sunny May morning. Christopher's mother, Virginia, snapped it through the kitchen window. Christopher sits cross-legged on the dandelion-studded grass while I perch on the driftwood seat under the gnarly apple tree that is just breaking into blossom. Ozzie has left Christopher's side and pads towards me across the shaggy lawn, his tail high and his head low, anticipating a nose rub.

I'm in a sleeveless T-shirt with my hair tied up, clear of my neck. The day lilies are knee-high; purple and yellow columbines nod, and the first green swords of iris leaf jab skyward. Looking at the photo I can almost smell the heavy, rich aroma of balm of Gilead, emanating from the opening cottonwood buds beside the cascading creek.

I think about the place where our front yard lay, smothered now under several metres of stony, infertile till. Do pockets remain underneath, even now, where life stirs? Does a sprig of Virginia creeper push blindly upwards seeking light? Did any of our trees remain rooted? Does the Japanese maple, or the old apple tree, still hear the call of spring and try to respond? After two years I know the answer is a resounding no. The giant eraser did its work too well.

And what of the beige filing cabinet and the precious treasures it held? All through that first year I scanned the deep gulley beside the house site whenever I went there, willing the filing cabinet to appear, certain that it would show itself. In December 2012, Duncan opened up the hole again and dug for four hours in the northwest corner (the bedroom area). I huddled with Christopher and Kurt in a biting wind off the lake, with a thin powder icing of snow etching the rough contours of the earthy hill. Nothing emerged.

On August 20, 2013, one year on, we tried for the last time. Glen Sorenson, an excavator operator from Glade, has family connections with Johnson's Landing and wanted to help the community. He offered five days of his excavator services at no charge. We requested six hours.

We were optimistic. We knew where the cabinet was *not*. Surely, by logical deduction we could track down a large lump of metal? The first dig in August 2012 had uncovered everything in its vicinity, including the wooden plank desk that lay on top of it, my desk stool and a box of onions that had stood on the bedroom floor right beside it.

The excavation team reunited for the day. Kurt brought his hoe. Lew, in his pith helmet, brought water. Christopher directed operations and explained the lay of the land to Glen. The large yellow excavator roared into life and bit into the earth near the corner of the house. Glen soon found the concrete external wall and dug systematically along its length, around the corner and down the west side of the house.

Again the bones and flesh of the tortured building showed themselves: splintered, rotting wood and congealed pink insulation. Deep, dark recesses of the basement and root cellar beckoned eerily and exuded a putrid stench. We made odd discoveries: an intact bottle of Pernod, its label almost illegible, had somehow rolled out of the root cellar. I picked up a rusted dress belt cast adrift from a distant bedroom drawer, a red embroidered housecoat, ripped and filthy, and one mouldy sandal from a pair I'd worn every summer.

The reopened tomb revealed countless visible reminders of our past life. Everything was still under there, for the most part quite recognizable. The intensely earthy smell that I'd loathed emanated even now from the freshly turned soil. To catch a whiff was to be catapulted back to those days of terror and grief.

After six hot and dusty hours, exhausted, horrified and unsettled by the hideousness, we gave up. The filing cabinet had seemingly evaporated. I'd brought along my collection of soft deer hide and silk bags, in which I'd planned to place the jewellery. How stupid I was to allow myself such high hopes. That evening, back in Kaslo, my eyes stinging with tears, I put the empty bags away.

I must make my peace with these last losses: my mother's rings, her gold necklace, the cultured pearls and my own small collection of jewellery that included gifts she had given me and loved to see me wear. They lie there still, somewhere under the mud. I visualize and speak to them, especially my mother's diamond and ruby engagement ring. I keep faith that they do not wish to remain lost from me forever. But there is nowhere left to search, and we will not excavate again.

As TIME PASSED, I began to see a larger picture—synchronicities within the two parallel threads of my personal story:

the losses in the landslides, and the losses that soon followed in England.

My mother was like a tiny boat bobbing far from shore on the high seas of vascular dementia when I went back to London in early October. She retained no short-term memory, yet was unerringly loving to everyone, and never forgot who her children were. Every day she asked fearfully how soon I'd be leaving again for Canada, and I'd say, "I've changed my ticket and I'm staying longer, much longer, this time." June's face would be wreathed in smiles and she'd squeeze my hand in her arthritic fingers. "Oh, that's *marvellous*, darling. I'm *so* glad! It means the world to me to have you here."

On sleepy days I sat in her room, sewing name tags into her clothes while she napped. On livelier days we watched her favourite afternoon TV game show, *Countdown*, and had tea together, just as we'd done so many times at home over the years. One day, watching *Countdown*, she astounded me by identifying an eight-letter word that I missed, as did the two contestants. Pretty good for advanced dementia! She said, "It just came to me," and I imagined my father perhaps whispering the word into her ear. June often said she sensed John's presence beside her, and he'd been an avid fan of *Countdown*.

My mother was so easy to kiss and caress. We held hands—she had the softest hands—and I brushed her hair. I'd never done these things on previous visits at her house, constrained by an almost physical barrier between us. At the onset of her dementia, June had been wound tight like a spring with nervous anxiety, panicky and unable to relax, endlessly repeating questions. Loneliness and depression were her constant attendants. And I expressed my guilt and worry through irritation. I was teacherly in my criticisms, coldly parental in my nagging. At the root of it I, too, was terrified of what might happen to her.

In the nursing home, with that barrier gone, I became a better daughter. I stroked my mother's hair back from her face as she lay on her bed under her blanket of knitted squares, ready for a nap, and covered her cheek in kisses. She giggled and gazed up at me, beautiful as a young girl again.

I hid a second secret from my mother, aside from not mentioning the landslides. My brother and I saw there was no realistic possibility that June would live independently again, so we decided to sell the family house. Andrew flew in from Australia, we put the house on the market and it sold in seventy-two hours. We started emptying the attic. I was grateful for the rare treat of having time alone with my "little brother," who lived half a world away.

We both noticed June's agitation at having so little cash in her wallet. She worried obsessively about paying for her care, her meals and our expenses. Andrew had the brilliant idea of photocopying a number of ten-pound notes and putting them in June's purse. She was happy again and seemed unaware that the notes were black and white instead of brown, and blank on the back. One day she gave me a grubby, well-fingered note and told me to go out and buy myself something special with it. I thanked her with a lump in my throat, and pasted the ten-pound note into my journal.

Andrew returned to Australia in mid-October and I buckled down to the huge task of dismantling thirty-six years of my parents' accumulation. Being of the pre–World War II generation, nothing was thrown away. Sheets were re-hemmed "sides-to-middle," and every last piece of string, elastic band and reusable envelope was kept.

There were days, I swear, when I almost wished for the purgative power of a cataclysmic event to sweep it all away! I spent painstaking hours poring over and sorting through ancient, dusty box files, folders, wads of letters, yellowing photographs, clothes and personal effects. In England, just three months on from the landslides, another era of my life drew inexorably towards its conclusion.

I reduced the London house to an empty shell. On the last morning I sat at the kitchen table, sensing a grief that swirled around me and seemed to emanate from the place itself. We were about to cut our connection. The day was bright. Sunbeams streamed across the deep burgundy carpet in the empty dining room.

I closed the front door, said goodbye to neighbours along the small terraced row of townhouses, then felt compelled to return and drink in each familiar detail, one last time. The characteristic *click* of the key in the lock. The distinctive smells: wool carpeting, central heating and a whiff of gas from the ancient cooker. Dust motes swam in the sunlit air. Then I caught the bus to my mother's nursing home.

I used the excuse of sickness to explain away my puffy, red-rimmed eyes and pale face. For reasons unfathomable, that day my mother kept insisting that it was high time we went home—we had to call a taxi right now. Was she somehow, subliminally, aware of the shift just made in the tectonic plates of her life?

On December 6, 2012, my last day in England, I thought my heart would break. My mother looked so pretty with her grey hair neatly brushed, wearing the new pink cardigan I'd bought her. I returned to her room after lunch to find three favourite nurses around her. Su, Lorna and Puja were helping June to write a birthday/Christmas card for me. June could no longer sign her name and was upset at the scrawl she made. But she managed big X's for kisses and O's for hugs. I fought back tears, hugged her and quietly slipped away before she realized that the dreaded moment had come to say goodbye.

I NEVER SAW my mother alive again. In February 2013, during a leg of my next journey to England, this time with Christopher, we learned that my mother had died unexpectedly. Fifteen hours after her death, Christopher and I stood in her small room at the nursing home. Her things lay scattered around as normal, but she herself was gone.

Christopher's presence lent me strength as we made funeral arrangements.

Grief is love that's become homeless, so they say. If we include my mother, and my family home in London, I guess I was left homeless three times in seven months. Things do tend to happen in threes.

Human beings are resilient. You think you'll never recover, and in some ways you don't—you are no longer the same person you were. But in time you move forward and forge a new path. We the bereaved are like war veterans whose legs and arms have been severed. Nothing can bring back the lost limbs, but we learn strategies to function around the losses.

I draw comfort from memory. I can always revisit the past and play my favourite scene over again, like a clip from a movie...

Drifting up to consciousness I squint at the clock: 6:45 a.m. I am cozy under the covers. A weight presses against my left leg. Ozzie is snuggled up close on his green and red knitted blanket.

My ears pick up the first sounds of the day: a scrunching of newspaper, a snapping of kindling sticks. A hatchet pounds rapidly through a block of cedar to make thin strips. *Tcheep, tcheep, tcheep.* Pause. I hear crackling in our basement wood stove. I won't get out of bed until the chimney starts ticking, then I'll know it's warm enough.

My eyes gradually gain long-distance focus. Through the window beside the bed a billow of woodsmoke gusts away between the trees and over the lake. A breezy day. I examine the tall firs just beyond the deck. If it's raining I'll see the pattern of drops against their dark boughs. No, the sky is brightening and it's going to be a beautiful day.

I gently ease my legs out of bed and slip a small pillow under the covers for Ozzie to lean against. His black forepaw is draped across his eyes to block the light and he's curled in a tight ball. He is not a morning cat. I lean forward to kiss between his ears and he raises his head groggily, his message clear: "Please go away!"

Across the room at my stand-up desk I switch on the MacBook and smile at the reassuring energy of its awakening C-major chord. The internet satellite receiver across the deck glows with three orange lights, signalling a good speed at which to download *The Guardian*, BBC podcasts and my email.

I wander downstairs to the basement and find Christopher gazing through the gold-framed glass door of the small Pacific Energy wood stove. We embrace and enquire how each of us slept. I sit next to him on the bottom step, mesmerized by the yellow and blue flames that lick at the wood and caress the ceiling of the stove box. Getting up, I toast myself, front and back, in the welcome radiant heat.

Upstairs I put the kettle on and make tea. Christopher joins me in the kitchen and we stand beside the tall picture window, lost in wonder at the expansive view southward down Kootenay Lake. He puts his arm around me with a quirky half-smile.

"Well babe, it's another tough day in paradise!"

John and Jillian Madill travelled an immense journey in one year. As a retired couple, they never expected to experience changes so abrupt and traumatic.

On July 12, 2013, one year to the day after the landslide, they slept in their own bed again for the first time. That was the day they retrieved their furniture from storage and brought it to their newly purchased permanent home—Ann MacNab's house in Howser, north of Kootenay Lake. The Howser community has been extremely welcoming and supportive of the couple.

Jillian told me, "I've said goodbye to Johnson's Landing. I don't feel any longing to go back there. Parts of it are still beautiful, but it's a difficult place to be. What you might long for is no longer there: no Petra, no Val and the girls. It was such a strong community, we all knew each other so well." Jillian was a long-time friend of Petra, who lived right next door. Val was also a nearby neighbour and friend. He and John always took care of waterline problems for south-side residents.

Jillian is stoic about the future. "I'm ready to move on, put it all behind us, work on this place, have some fun. And not think about the landslide all the time. I think we'll be happy here. A lot of it is your attitude: we can mourn forever for Johnson's Landing or we can get on with it. And we just have to get on with it."

KATE O'KEEFE IDENTIFIED three big losses: "First, the immediate loss of the people who died. Second, the loss of the people who no longer live here, and that's different—Jillian and you are still alive but we have a changed relationship now. And thirdly, there's the loss of geography: the scar that will deface this land forever. And the loss of greatest magnitude for me is the last one. The new landscape dictates every turn and decision I make. If I walk north I am walking 'towards the slide.' If I walk south I am walking 'away from the slide.' I cannot easily walk to the beach. It's all about the slide. I can never forget it."

Jillian and John's decision was made for them: they had no option but to leave. It was the same for Rachel, Christopher and me. But Kate and Harvey had a choice because their main home, Algot Johnson's old cabin, lies safely to the south of the evacuation zone. "It was really hard, but we've made the decision to stay. I have a beautiful life here and we are doing good things: installing solar energy and our own water system; Harvey moved his workshop and will get his pottery studio up and running again. But the place will never be what it was."

For Harvey Armstrong, the enormity of the event took

months to sink in and, like so many residents, he floundered for the first year. His property and buildings had forty years of memories attached to them, and he'd intended to leave the land to his sons.

In Harvey's opinion, the community felt split and conflicted, physically divided by Gar Creek and fractured by disagreements over water issues and access to property. But he believes Johnson's Landing will heal eventually. "It is too wonderful and beautiful a place not to heal. People will come who don't have our background. Wherever you live in the mountains you have to deal with these events. All over the Kootenays people are facing weather-related threats. Johnson's Landing just happened to be one of the first and one of the biggest."

For Renata Klassen, the elapse of time has helped her grief run its course. "You need the passage of the seasons, the familiarity of each one, until the first year is done. Then another year starts and you have a measure. I sought help, did intensive trauma work, then I saw Millie at Community Services weekly for eight weeks, her last eight weeks in Kaslo, and I felt so thankful. She gave me some psychological tools to work with after she left. My dog Lennie died in mid-August 2013, and his death brought me extreme clarity around a number of things. I continue to seek the help I need."

Susan VanRooy and Bob Yetter are determined not to abandon their home and their hopes for a renewal of community life. Susan told me, "We will move on. Something has changed irretrievably, but change is inevitable. It's part of the circle of life. Hopefully something positive will come out of it for all of us."

Before the landslides, Susan used to pause during her morning run, just above Creek Corner in the Gar Creek draw. She'd meditate and draw strength from the powerful force of the water surging past her. A cedar tree stood on a tiny, mossy island in the stream, its roots spanning the channel. Susan would jump onto the island and rest on the curved bough of the cedar tree, sometimes hearing a winter wren's song, in this beautiful green place of solace. She was often there, in the middle of Gar Creek, at ten thirty in the morning. If she'd been in Johnson's Landing that fateful day, with the high water roaring, would she have heard the landslide coming?

"Now there's a sign on the road that says: NO STOPPING. I feel a sense of dread, but I'm trying to make friends with the new creek. It will be beautiful again one day."

LILA TAYLOR TOLD me she's doing well, although the first year was gruelling. She learned a lot about who she was and how to take care of herself. "I'm still upset sometimes, and still miss Diana. It comes back, but less often. I try to focus on the good memories. Life goes forward in honour of the ones who died. With young death it makes you want to live more fully. Everything looks more intense and beautiful and interesting. If you're doing something you don't like, then stop! It's a waste of time. You need to enjoy every moment."

On the first anniversary of the disaster Margie and Lila joined other friends in the Landing, including Rachel and Diana's mother, Lynn Migdal, from Florida. Eighteen people met at the site of the Webbers' house, around a heart-shaped firepit. At exactly 10:37 a.m. they held hands around the circle, then spoke prayers, told stories, sang songs and played percussion instruments. Lynn passed tequila and a tray of chocolate and halva around the group to signify the bitter and the sweet.

The afternoon saw a simple commemoration on the beach: a gathering, a moment of silence, then a scattering of flower petals over the water and a floating altar adorned with flowers. Margie went into our abandoned garden at my request, and put flowers on Ozzie's grave beside the mulberry tree.

Margie, Lila, Tenise Trueman (one of Rachel Webber's best friends) and Louis Bockner stayed overnight on the beach, singing songs to Louis's guitar, reminiscing about childhood days and keeping a vigil.

I asked Margie how she felt.

"It's so tough to lose four people. But it is also hard to lose this land. It's always been home to me and is such a special place for so many of us—it's almost like losing another person. Shared experience, even when it's tragic, creates a special connection between people. How long it takes or how it happens, I don't know, but I believe Johnson's Landing will heal."

LYNN MIGDAL TOLD me from her home in Florida, "I think the key to living through multiple sudden death, destruction of one's home and dream is best said by Joel Osteen: 'You do not move forward with your dreams unless your dreams are more powerful than your painful past.' I have a dream to lift the consciousness of the world into a peaceful place, and to spread the truth about natural healing and global warming. I have always wanted to save the children of the world, and it is this mission that gets me up every day, helping others with chiropractic and ChiroChi, and giving workshops on natural healing.

"I am starting to include in my workshops the message that suffering is a choice. And we get to choose how long during the day we do it. The techniques that keep me emotionally fit during this horrible time are chiropractic, acupuncture, massage and breath work. I found out early in the grieving process that I had to choose some quality time to 'feel' my feelings, and lie down if I was sobbing. Lying down and breathing while crying is actually healing."

PATRICK STEINER AND Colleen O'Brien, who stayed on their farm, suffered serious economic hardship following the landslides. "Our farm was affected pretty drastically. We lost approximately $20,000 worth of crops in 2012. We lost many seed crops, so had less to offer our customers, and much less bulk for retail orders. An online campaign started on our behalf raised approximately $9,000.

"Our 2013 has been as tough as last year, and we're finding it extremely difficult. We've had to deal with water maintenance issues, and there's still no permanent water system in place. Other things we're struggling with include turning this property into a viable farm—it's rocky, sloped and infertile—to be able to produce the quantity and quality we're used to, and the lack of infrastructure on our farm.

"We feel less sure about Johnson's Landing as a long-term place for us. The landslide highlighted challenges and difficulties with living out here. Raising a child, we have to go long distances for support—doctor, clothes, play group—and it takes a great deal of time out of the day. We are trying to improve the house and property but it is a lot of work. We feel fortunate because Kaslo and the north Kootenay Lake communities were really supportive and helpful after the slide. In a less close-knit place this disaster would have been much harder to get through."

ROGER AND CAROL differed in their feelings about Johnson's Landing, one year on. Roger said, "I don't feel happy here. The nature of the place has changed. I have no fear of more landslides—the risk is probably minimal. But it used to be a magical place, almost another world, a place I was content never to leave. Now it's a paradise lost. If I were not embroiled in things here and had the choice to move elsewhere, I would do so. The 'real' Johnson's Landing is nothing but a memory."

Carol said, "It is not the same magical place it was before, but it is still pretty special. I enjoy being here. Before, nobody knew where Johnson's Landing was. Now everyone knows. The first year was very stressful for everyone and recovery takes time. Who knows? The community could become even better."

Kurt Boyer decided in 2013 to move back to his house beside Gar Creek. "I love my life and work here. If some freaky thing happens, and I'm making too much noise to hear it, and the mud takes me, so be it. I'll die doing what I love."

Kurt's decision to move back home was cemented when the provincial government refused to buy people out. The DFA program offered him $37,000 compensation if he would first destroy his home-cum-workshop—a vastly insufficient sum with which to purchase anything else. So he decided to stay and take his chances. DFA funded his replacement waterline. "The gods were smiling on me," he concluded with a smile.

Gail Spitler is worried about Johnson's Landing. Some areas are too hazardous for human habitation but others are safe, although property values have all been affected by the stigma of the landslide. How will the community keep functioning? Will new people move to the Landing, attracted by the cheap land?

Gail believes the climate is changing. Heavy rainfalls started in the 1990s and the extreme weather events are ever more alarming. "I think this is just the beginning," she told me. The local government has not done much to educate the public about landslide risks except to issue a fact sheet about "hazard indicators." In Gail's opinion it will have to do much more in the future.

Johnson's Landing used to feel like an extended family, big enough to allow for all its quirky characters to express themselves without impinging on neighbours. Gail worries that the current population is so reduced in size that healthy community life may be more difficult going forward.

Lynne Cannon struggled in the aftermath of the slides. "I'm still in recovery, not there yet. I feel dislocated and alone. I am called, by some, one of the 'unaffected,' but the losses were immeasurable and one grapples all the time with changes in the community; the landslide is always in your face. At times I wish I could be a hermit. I lack the resilience to go out into the world and be myself. But you can only move forward. And we're not about to leave Johnson's Landing."

During the first year, Rachel Rozzoni returned to her ravaged house every few weeks. "The house was a shell, with rat and mouse shit everywhere. No power—the fridge and freezer leaked all over the floor. It felt so ugly."

Rachel would lose herself in a task, then look up. "Holy shit! Look where I am!" The landslide had swirled around three sides of the house, and was visible from every corner of the property. Rachel's chores always seemed to take longer than planned and she'd become so upset she'd leave without completing her list.

Adding insult to injury, in March 2013 thieves broke into several buildings on properties devastated by the landslide, including Rachel's garage. "They made a real mess. They took tools, the ladder we needed to get into the house, hoses, an old computer..." Some of the stolen goods were later dumped on the road on the Argenta Flats, but Rachel never saw a list of what was returned and retrieved nothing.

Now she's in school, studying online for a qualification in midwifery. She wanted to focus on a path, she said, even though it's costing "a ton of money." It felt important, and was something she had to do for herself.

In August 2013, Loran Godbe told me he feels differently about his long-time home. "Johnson's Landing is changed forever. It was a wonderful place, but I don't feel comfortable, wondering what's up the mountain. It's a daily trauma. Every time I look at the creek a blast of adrenalin goes through me. It's not good to live with that kind of stress." Loran reacts traumatically to the sounds of rumbling trucks and thunder.

Loran and Linda moved to Trail, three hours' drive away, on account of Linda's need for regular kidney dialysis, but have since moved back to the Landing; Linda returns every week for treatment. It's been hard for them both. As Loran put it, "Trail's a city and we're not city people. I've lived surrounded by wilderness all my life. I'm used to walking outside in the morning with grass under my bare feet, and preparing for the day's many projects and activities on our little farm."

Gerry stayed behind at their house in the Landing, with only a generator for power for more than a year. With Linda and Loran gone with the car, Gerry relied on others to bring fuel, food and the horse's feed. In the days before the road was rebuilt he reached the horse via a strenuous journey that took four hours, twice a day. He hiked to the shore below Carol and Roger's, paddled his canoe out through the log-jam to the south beach, then climbed the hill to Kootenay Joe Road, packing water in buckets from Kate and Harvey's pond for the horse.

Due to our chaotic lives in the first weeks after the slides, Christopher and I kept in touch with Virginia Klassen, his mom, only sporadically. Virginia told me, "Rationally, I understood why you didn't call. But emotionally, I felt abandoned. I wanted so badly to be up there with you. I wanted to be in the car going back with Christopher that Thursday evening. It was like my home."

Virginia saw huge change in her granddaughter, Margie Smith. "Margie had stayed with me for several months two years earlier, when Diana Webber was also in Eugene. In fact we celebrated Diana's twenty-first birthday here. When Margie came back here after the landslide, she was in deep grief for the Webber family, especially Diana, and I was reminded of what I learned when my son Michael died.

"Each person's experience of, and reaction to, trauma is unique. The grief is so overpowering that often there's no strength left to extend empathy and care to others in the family or group, and people feel abandoned. Relatives or friends who live far away may be just as impacted as those living near the disaster.

"There's a sense of losing not just material things and the present way of life, but also the future—growing old together in a familiar, beloved setting; plans and dreams; and the contributions that the people who died could have made."

BOBBI HUBER, IN Birchdale, feels hopeful for the future. She and Peter often hike in Switzerland and have seen many slide zones in the Swiss Alps. Little signs announce that a village was buried or badly damaged by a landslide, perhaps several hundred years ago. "This does happen, all over the world. People go on, but it's going to take time."

She believes the community will heal. "There will be 'before the slide' and 'after the slide.' This is a huge event that, ultimately, will bind people together. It creates a common history and makes the community stronger."

THE GEOTECHNICAL REPORT put both of Osa Thatcher's properties partially within the high hazard zone. "This leaves me perplexed," she told me. "I can't rent out a house that's in a high hazard zone. Yet the upkeep has to be done and the taxes paid."

In monetary terms, Osa lost everything. But she says the real value of her properties lies in what they hold and mean to her. The spirit of the place lives on in her woodlot—a mixed forest of pine, birch and larch—as well as in her wonderful neighbours, and in her garden, which grows good corn and tomatoes. The hillside is south facing, there are no mosquitoes and the beach is beautiful. She and Paul visit from their house in Kaslo as often as they can.

Osa still sees much to be thankful for and enjoy. "The landslides were just another glitch in the saga. The Landing will live on. It is such a beautiful place."

It's a comfort to know where Ozzie lies buried, a place we can return to.

Acknowledgements

THROUGHOUT THE SUMMER of 2012 Christopher and I were sustained thanks to countless thoughtful and generous gifts bestowed by friends and strangers alike in the communities of Johnson's Landing, Argenta, Kaslo, Nelson and beyond. Family members and friends overseas also rallied to our aid. There are too many of you to name individually, but I want you to know how much it meant to us. You created a safety net of support, love and caring in those dark and painful days.

Paul Hunter and Osa Thatcher have been our close friends for more than two decades, through good times and in adversity. They grounded and anchored us with their reassuring presence. Thank you both.

Special thanks also to Gail Spitler and Lynne Cannon. Gail, a wonderful teacher and adviser, quickly resolved every computer glitch. Gail was the first person (after Christopher and Holley, my editor) to read the manuscript; she is a leadership figure in Johnson's Landing and I was reassured to have her ringing endorsement. I thank Lynne Cannon for creating a sanctuary in Johnson's Landing where I could feel safe, nurtured and at peace. Gail and Lynne's beautiful home, and our enduring friendship over many years, formed my bridge back to Johnson's Landing after the disaster.

I acknowledge with gratitude the financial and other assistance we received after the landslides from the British Columbia provincial government through their Emergency

Social Services and Disaster Financial Assistance programs, and from the Canadian Red Cross.

Thank you to the thirty-five people who agreed to be interviewed for this book: for your willingness to relive that painful time and tell me your stories. What storytellers we have in our midst! I am humbled by your trust in me. Of course, any errors in the recounting of your stories are mine alone.

Holley Rubinsky, my writing mentor and editor, assisted me through five drafts of the manuscript as the book's eventual form gradually emerged out of the content. Holley taught me how to write a book and I am deeply grateful for her enthusiastic commitment and editorial expertise. I learned immensely from our collaboration.

Thank you, Louis Bockner, for your assistance with photography for the book. And to others who generously offered me pictures: Gail Spitler, Lynne Campbell, Lynne March, Renata Klassen, Margaret Smith, Greg Utzig, Kurt Boyer, Lew McMillan, Zan Mautner, Doug Pyper, Lynn Migdal and Christopher Klassen.

To the inestimable Morty Mint, my literary agent: thank you for your encouragement and faith in the project.

My heartfelt thanks to everyone at Harbour Publishing for your support of this writing project and for your professionalism and expertise in bringing it to fruition. You were delightful to work with.

Finally, I want to thank my husband, Christopher, for his unwavering support, even when it meant no supper prepared and the house neglected! I thank the universe that our lives were spared so that we could grieve and remember our past together. There is comfort in memories shared. Christopher's recollections and perspective on our experience have greatly enriched this memoir.

Index

PHOTO: LOUIS BOCKNER

About the Author

AMANDA BATH WAS born and raised in England, and lived in London before moving to the tiny community of Johnson's Landing, BC, in 1993. She holds a Ph.D. in Catalan Literature and worked in human rights research for Amnesty International for a decade. Since her home in Johnson's Landing was destroyed by the 2012 landslides, she now lives in Kaslo, BC, with her husband Christopher Klassen.